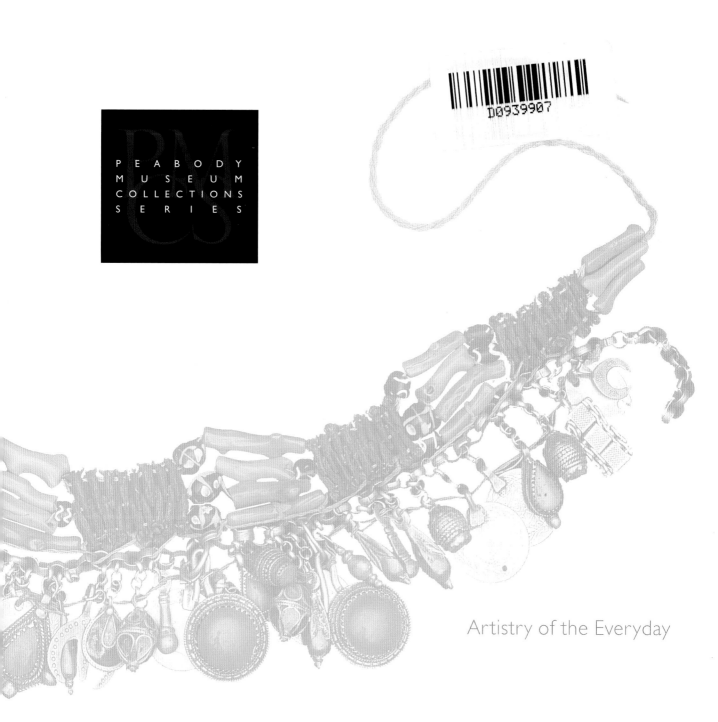

PEABODY
MUSEUM
COLLECTIONS
SERIES

Artistry of the Everyday

ARTISTRY OF THE EVERYDAY

Beauty and Craftsmanship in Berber Art

Lisa Bernasek

Foreword by Susan Gilson Miller

Photographs by Hillel S. Burger and Mark Craig

Rubie Watson, Series Editor

Peabody Museum Press, Harvard University

Editorial direction by Joan K. O'Donnell
Copyediting by Jane Kepp
Series design by Kristina Kachele Design, llc
Cover and text design by Kristina Kachele Design, llc, and Karen Mazur
Composition by Karen Mazur
Production management by Donna Dickerson
Proofreading by Deborah Boehm and Donna Dickerson
Digital prepress by Jay's Publishers Services, Inc.
Printed and bound in China by Oceanic Graphic Printing

ISBN 978-0-87365-405-0

Library of Congress Cataloging-in-Publication Data:

Bernasek, Lisa, 1975–
Artistry of the everyday : beauty and craftsmanship in Berber art / Lisa Bernasek ; foreword by Susan Gilson Miller ; photographs by Hillel S. Burger and Mark Craig.
p. cm. — (Peabody Museum collections series)
Includes bibliographical references.
ISBN-13: 978-0-87365-405-0 (pbk. : alk. paper)
1. Berbers—Material culture—Exhibitions. 2. Berbers—Social life and customs—Exhibitions. 3. Arts, Berber—Exhibitions. 4. Peabody Museum of Archaeology and Ethnology. I. Peabody Museum of Archaeology and Ethnology. II. Title. DT 193.5.B45B47 2008
730.089'933—dc22
                                        2007047873

This book is printed on acid-free paper.

FRONTISPIECE: Berber design motifs. Clockwise from top left: Details of serving dish (PM 46-40-50/5960, see pl. 5), woman's cape (PM 41-34-50/5420, see pl. 9), and woman's traveling bag (PM 975-32-50/11911, see pl. 24). Photographs 98520079, 98520071, 98520092, and 98520091 by Mark Craig © by the President and Fellows of Harvard College.

COVER: Clove necklace, PM 46-40-50/5962. Photograph 98520082 by Mark Craig © by the President and Fellows of Harvard College.

Contents

Illustrations

PLATES

Chez les Berbères . . . l'art n'apparaît pas comme une activité supérieure, où seule une élite est capable d'accéder. Il est le compagnon familier de la vie des hommes, si humble soit-elle. Entre l'utile et le beau, nulle opposition, mais une union constante.

Among the Berbers . . . art does not appear as a superior activity, which only an elite is able to access. It is a familiar companion in the life of men, humble though it may be. Between the useful and the beautiful there is no opposition, but a constant union.

—Henri Terrasse and Jean Hainaut, *Les Arts Décoratifs au Maroc*, 1925 (author's translation)

High Atlas village, Valley of Imilchil, Morocco. Photograph by Steffen Pierce © 1986 Steffen Pierce.

Berber Art and Identity

Susan Gilson Miller

BERBER IS HARDLY A HOUSEHOLD WORD in the United States. For many of us, Berbers and Berber arts are difficult to locate culturally and geographically, but Berbers are indeed alive and well. They form a vibrant social, political, and cultural community today, not only in North Africa, where they have lived for millennia, but also in Europe and the Americas. They are farmers, shopkeepers, university professors, hairdressers, government officials, writers of fiction and poetry, craftspeople, filmmakers, military officers, and peace activists. They live in Tizi Ouzou, Rabat, Paris, London, Hoboken, and Orange County, and they share a sense of Berber identity, held together through a memory of common roots and strong linguistic, social, and cultural bonds.

My first experience of Berber culture came many years ago in Morocco, when I was in search of a housekeeper to take care of my two young children so I could spend part of each day working in an archive. The neighborhood grapevine brought a young woman to my door. She was shy but friendly, her face etched with a delicate tracery of blueish tattoos. Her name was Mbaraka, and she came from the mountainous region known as the Rif. During the three years she was in our employ, she gave me a graduate education in Berber arts. Mbaraka made our *qanūn*, or charcoal brazier, an essential piece of household equipment; she cooked couscous with a finesse rivaling that of the finest chefs of the Royal Palace; she taught me Moroccan Arabic with the patience of a saint. She also instructed me in the *qā'ida*, the code of behavior that covers the fundamentals of social decorum, usually passed from parent to child in the course of a generation. She transmitted this information by example and with a generosity that was humbling. Like Carleton Coon's companion Limnibhy, of whom Lisa Bernasek writes in these pages, Mbaraka was my friend and confidante, my teacher and inform‑ant, my surrogate parent and my client. Ours was a complicated relationship that last‑ed for many years. When she died in 2004, I had gifts to remember her by: a heavy brass mortar and pestle, a silver bangle, and an agate ring, the stone tinted red from henna.

It would have been difficult at the time to sort out exactly what was "Berber" about the education Mbaraka gave me. The Berber component of North African life is so intertwined with the rest that it is sometimes difficult to unravel. In the twentieth cen‑tury, French social scientists, working hand‑in‑glove with colonial administrators, closely studied the rural tribal groupings in French‑ruled Morocco and Algeria that spoke some form of Tamazight, the Berber name for their own language. Using ancient tactics of divide and rule, colonial authorities deployed this information to convince Berbers of their dissimilarity to Arabs. Working with sparse ethnographic knowledge but a heavy dose of noblesse oblige, they categorized Berbers as lost cousins of European origin, thinly Islamicized, and hence eminently suitable for co‑optation as junior partners in the imperial enterprise. Ultimately these efforts failed, for Berbers were as vehement as the rest of the population about the inadmissibility of foreign rule. As combatants in the wars of independence, they stood alongside their Arab counterparts, placing their hopes in the state‑to‑be and making equal sacrifices in the cause of freedom.

False characterizations were only the beginning of the problem of gaining recogni‑tion of Berber difference. When the wheel inevitably turned and independence arrived in the 1950s and 1960s, a new impediment arose in the form of Arab national‑ism and its emphasis on the Arab origins of all North African peoples, including Berbers. Berber specificity was historically erased when nationalist historians con‑strued them as an Arabian tribe who had wandered far afield, reaching North Africa in the vanguard of the Arab invasion. The recognition of Berber language and culture was brushed aside as an unneeded complication in the rush to build the image of the homogeneous Arab nation. Determined to create a united front against the return of the colonizer, newly independent Moroccan and Algerian regimes dismissed out of hand the notion of a separate and meaningful Berber identity.

Not until 1980, under pressure from spontaneous uprisings in Berber areas of Algeria and in the face of mounting demands for political liberalization in Morocco, did North African states first publicly acknowledge Berber cultural rights. The door opened, at first just a crack, and then more widely. By the year 2000 a full-scale cultural revival was under way, led by mushrooming Berber cultural associations in North Africa, France, and the United States. The North African states grasped the extent of popular feeling behind these movements and tried to direct them. Berber activism is now officially institutionalized in organizations such as the Moroccan Institut Royal de la Culture Amazighe (IRCAM), whose stated goal is to "safeguard and promote the Amazigh (Berber) culture and language." Now integrated into the national agenda in both Morocco and Algeria, Berber activism grows apace, but always under the watchful eye of the state.

Meanwhile, the public debate over what exactly constitutes Berber cultural identity continues. The Peabody Museum exhibition "Imazighen! Beauty and Artisanship in Berber Life" was conceived in the spirit of this ongoing debate. In curating the exhibition, Lisa Bernasek and I set out to explore one of the key contexts in which the current Berber cultural renaissance has unfolded—the area of artistic production—by highlighting outstanding examples from the Peabody collection.

With few curatorial skills to go on, we prowled the Peabody's storage rooms and rediscovered hundreds of everyday objects of the sorts we had become familiar with during our North African years. The variety was breathtaking. Soon the objects we identified for display began to take on lives of their own, emerging as distinct entities, telling us stories about women's work in Kabylia, Tuareg codes of honor, and other themes described in the pages of this book. The exhibition opened at the Peabody in December 2004.

Lisa Bernasek has taken this material and turned it into a beautiful catalogue that will endure beyond the exhibition. With her in-depth knowledge of North Africa, she was well suited to the task. Lisa spent two years in a village near the town of Rissani in southeastern Morocco as a Peace Corps volunteer. Many of the everyday objects seen in this book—water jugs, serving platters, and clay vessels used in food preparation—were part of the furniture of that life. An understanding of their ordinariness, coupled with a profound appreciation of the care and taste with which they were crafted, was just one of the gifts Lisa brought to this project.

Another asset was her training as an anthropologist, which gave her the interpretive skills needed to create hierarchies within the collection. She was able to see connections, identify objects most worthy of study, and devise readings that were both scientific and accessible. Finally, her ability as a historian added an unexpected dimension to the project. Although many anthropologists write about history, Lisa does so with flair and inspiration, skillfully drawing comparisons that are driven by curiosity and attention to telling detail.

This catalogue brings to English-speaking audiences a rich sampling of the beauty, diversity, and breadth of Berber arts. The chosen objects are representative of an independent Berber consciousness that has developed over the centuries. Berber arts must be acknowledged in their own right as a vibrant expression of a people who are heirs to a unique historical experience. Given the mysterious ways in which culture moves around the world nowadays, this catalogue is a durable contribution to a movement that began in North Africa and Europe and has now reached the United States. The aim of the project was to introduce the treasures of the Peabody into an expanding global discourse about Berber cultural identity. I am especially proud that the museum and its staff understood the value of this aspiration and that Lisa Bernasek has translated it into a reality.

ACKNOWLEDGMENTS

THIS BOOK GREW OUT OF an exhibition I curated with Susan Gilson Miller, director of the Moroccan Studies Program and senior lecturer on Islamic Civilizations at Harvard. Susan and I worked closely together to develop themes, choose objects, and write display text, and much of this volume is directly indebted to her efforts. She was also an important mentor throughout the curating of the exhibit and the writing of the book, and I am extremely grateful for her guidance and unfailing generosity in reading and commenting on many versions of the text. The manuscript was also greatly improved through the thoughtful comments of Jane Goodman and an anonymous reader. Rubie Watson and Joan K. O'Donnell were patient and insightful editors, providing direction and ideas at critical points. The text also benefited from Jane Kepp's careful copyediting. Any remaining flaws are my responsibility.

I am also indebted to the designers, illustrators, and photographers who made this such a beautiful book. I am especially pleased that the late Hillel S. Burger was able to do so much of the photography, one of the last projects he undertook for the Peabody Museum. I have admired his photographs of the Peabody's collections for many years and know that he will be greatly missed.

Research for the exhibit and book took place over many years and involved more people than I can name here, to all of whom I am extremely grateful. Many members of the Peabody Museum staff facilitated Susan Miller's and my research on objects and photographs and in the archives. I especially thank Nynke Dorhout Jolly, Sam Tager, and Donna Dickerson, who shepherded us through the creation of the exhibit and provided valuable insights at every stage. Kristi Marks served as a research assistant for the project in the summer of 2004, and her contributions to image selection and object research are directly represented in this volume. I also carried out research using the Carleton S. Coon Papers at the National Anthropological Archives of the Smithsonian Institution and the Charles P. Bowditch family papers at the Massachusetts Historical Society. Staff at both these institutions were extremely helpful. Eleanor Briggs provided information about her father's collecting and research activities. Many other scholars, organizations, and individuals in the United States, Morocco, and France helped in numerous ways during the research and writing, and I am grateful for the information and suggestions they provided.

Generous support for the exhibition on which this book is based was provided by the Moroccan Studies Program at Harvard University, with support from the Moroccan Ministry of Higher Education, the Center for Middle Eastern Studies at Harvard University, and the Briggs Fund for the Peabody Museum for Exhibition of Materials from the Berber Culture. Steven C. Caton, director of the Center for Middle Eastern Studies, was an invaluable champion of the entire undertaking, and I am grateful for his support of my participation in it. I also thank Rubie Watson and Bill Fash, who served as directors of the Peabody Museum over the course of the project, for their early and continued support of both the exhibit and the book.

Many colleagues and friends also supported me in completing this project. Chris Stone and Louis Le Pen read early versions of the chapters and provided insightful comments that helped shape the final drafts. Louis Le Pen, my husband, has been a continuous source of encouragement throughout the project. I want especially to acknowledge my parents, who have been unfailingly supportive of the travels and explorations that have contributed to my interest in the arts of North Africa.

NOTE ON TRANSLITERATION

IN TRANSCRIBING BERBER AND ARABIC WORDS, I have aimed to strike a balance between accuracy and accessibility for a general audience. For geographical and personal names, I have relied on standard English reference sources. One exception is in the chapter devoted to the Rif, where I have used Carleton Coon's spellings for the names of his Riffian companions. Arabic words are transliterated according to the system of the *International Journal of Middle East Studies*, except where an accepted English form of the word exists (for example, "jellaba"). In transliterating Berber words I have attempted to follow current scholarly practice for the varieties of Berber in each of the three regions I discuss, although in certain cases I have simplified the orthography in order not to burden readers with too many diacritics and special characters. I hope this system, though less precise than a rigorous transliteration, will give readers an exposure to the Berber language.[1]

Notes on specific characters:
ᶜ represents the pharyngeal consonant called *ᶜain* in Arabic.
' represents the glottal stop called *hamza* in Arabic.

dh is equivalent to the *th* sound in *father*.

gh is the voiced velar fricative, similar to the French *r* and called *ghain* in Arabic. It is often transcribed as γ in current Berber scholarship.

x is the voiceless velar fricative, equivalent to the German *ch*. It is also transcribed as *kh* in certain cases in this volume.

A dot under a letter indicates an emphatic consonant.

A line over a letter indicates an elongated vowel.

Artistry of the Everyday

National (Kabylie)

Mountain path in Kabylia, late nineteenth century. Photograph probably purchased in Algeria in 1902; donated by the heirs of Charles P. Bowditch in 1946. PM 2004.29.11124.

The Imazighen and Their Arts

THE PEABODY MUSEUM OF ARCHAEOLOGY AND ETHNOLOGY is deservedly famous for its archaeological and ethnographic collections from the Americas, but hidden in its vast storerooms lie other treasures from around the world. A visit to these back rooms is like a trip across the continents and through the centuries, and each object one sees is likely to have a fascinating story behind it. This is certainly true of the Peabody's collections from the Berber regions of North Africa. If these objects could speak for themselves, they could tell us much more about their life histories than can be derived from museum records, collectors' notes, and secondary litera-ture. But using such sources, researchers can piece together some of the stories sur-rounding the objects, their makers, and their collectors, revealing a great deal about both specific objects' trajectories and the larger world of Berber arts, history, and culture.

The Peabody's collections from Berber North Africa came to the museum not as part of a systematic effort to create a "Berber collection" but as a result of various people's interests in North Africa and the Peabody Museum. The more than 450 pieces from Berber regions in Algeria and Morocco now housed at the museum were acquired by both travelers and Harvard-trained anthropologists. The majority of the objects were made and collected in the late nineteenth or early twentieth century, and many of them had been used in daily life before they were acquired by the eventual donor to the Peabody. In a way these are ordinary objects—blankets, clothing, storage vessels, utensils, bags—but they are also intricately decorated works of art that showcase the talents of individual craftsmen and craftswomen.

Like most other museum collections, the Peabody's collection of Berber art does not make up a complete catalogue of forms, designs, or regions. Rather, it offers glimpses of Berber artisanship and life at different times and in different places, a portrayal of Berber culture that is necessarily selective and incomplete. The collection largely represents three regions where Berber speakers live: Kabylia, in northeastern Algeria; the Rif, in northern Morocco; and the Tuareg territories of the Algerian Sahara.[2] These chapters and the accompanying plates provide greater detail about the objects, the people who made them, and the travelers and anthropologists who collected them. First, I want to sketch out who the Berbers are and what is meant by "Amazigh" arts.

When writing about North African history and culture, defining who or what is "Berber" is a tricky matter, one that has occupied scholars for centuries.[3] At the most basic level one can say that the people now known as Berbers—*Imazighen*, in the Berber language—are the descendants of the original inhabitants of North Africa. (*Amazigh* is the singular noun and adjective form.) From at least 7000 B.C.E. these peoples occupied a territory stretching from the Canary Islands to western Egypt and from the Mediterranean coast to the farthest reaches of the Sahara. Today Imazighen continue to live dispersed across North Africa, though often in the more isolated Saharan and mountainous regions, where they have best been able to preserve their language and cultural traditions.

The largest Berber communities are found in Algeria and Morocco, where Arabic is the official language. Until recently these states emphasized the Arab and Islamic aspects of their national cultural identity and downplayed the Berber component.

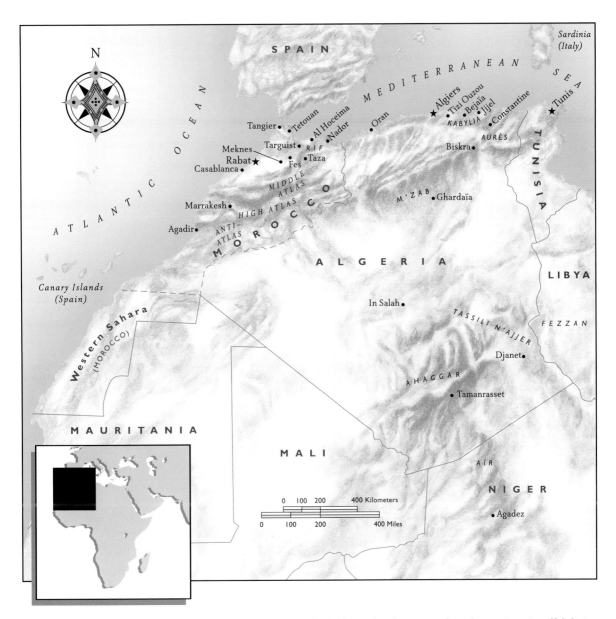

Northwest Africa, including key places mentioned in the text. The Peabody Museum's collections are from three main regions: Kabylia in northeastern Algeria, the Rif in northern Morocco, and the Ahaggar region of southern Algeria, home to the Kel Ahaggar Tuareg. Map by Deborah Reade.

The Imazighen and Their Arts   5

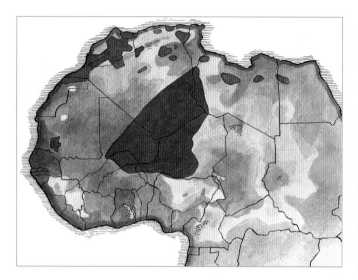

The areas of North Africa in which a variety of Berber is the first language of much of the population today (shown in red). Detail of a map by Leslie Evans, courtesy Leslie Evans.

Although no official population figures exist for these countries, estimates generally place the number of Berbers today at 20 to 25 percent of the Algerian population of almost 33 million and at 40 percent of the Moroccan population of just over 33 million. The Tuareg, a Berber-speaking people who live spread across the Saharan portions of Niger, Mali, Burkina Faso, Algeria, and Libya, total approximately 1 million persons. Smaller communities that have remained Berber speaking can be found in Tunisia, northwestern Libya, the Siwa oasis in Egypt, and southern Mauritania. In addition, many Berbers have migrated to Europe and North America. Among people of Algerian origin in France, for example, approximately one-third are from Berber regions.[4]

Besides identifying Berbers today according to people's historical connections to specific territories, scholars often use a linguistic definition: a Berber is someone who speaks a variety of the Berber language as a mother tongue. Berber is part of the Afro-Asiatic language family, which also includes the Semitic languages and ancient Egyptian. It was well established in North Africa by the second millennium B.C.E. Today people speak Berber in regional varieties that share many linguistic features but are not always mutually comprehensible.[5]

In recent years Berber linguists have begun to standardize Berber into a more formal written and spoken, pan-regional language called Tamazight. Although Berber has been primarily a spoken language throughout its history, Berber inscriptions in an ancient Libyan alphabet dating to at least the fourth century B.C.E. have been found in archaeological sites dispersed across North Africa. This ancient alphabet is related to the Tifinagh alphabet, used until recently only by the Saharan Tuareg (pl. 1). Tifinagh, too, has been standardized in recent years and is now being used to teach Tamazight in Moroccan public schools. Berber poets, writers, and journalists sometimes also use the Latin or the Arabic script when they write in Berber.

North Africa and its indigenous inhabitants have long been part of the Mediterranean circulation of peoples, goods, technologies, and ideas, and Imazighen have lived alongside other people originating outside of North Africa since ancient times. Phoenicians, Romans, Vandals, and Byzantines preceded Arabs, Ottoman Turks, and Europeans. These foreigners controlled and influenced Berber regions to varying degrees, but throughout history the Berbers maintained their language and many of their cultural traditions even as they adopted aspects of the newcomers' ways of life. The most significant adoption was that of Islam, which Arab invaders brought to North Africa in the seventh and eighth centuries C.E. Despite the Berbers' fierce resistance to Arab rule, Islam eventually took hold, and Berbers became important actors in spreading the new religion throughout North Africa and into the Iberian Peninsula. Indeed, the great dynasties of medieval North Africa—the Almoravids, Almohads, and Marinids—all arose from Berber origins. Islam continues to be the religion of the majority of Berber speakers today, although a tradition of secularism also exists among Amazigh political activists.

Over the course of their long history, the Berbers have received different names from the peoples who came into contact with them. They appear as Libyans in ancient Egyptian records, as Garamantes in Herodotus's chronicles, and as Numidians in writings from the time of the Phoenicians' rule over Carthage. The origins of the word *Berber* are debated, but most scholars agree that it derives from the Latin *barbarus* (Greek *barbaroi*), a term the Romans applied to certain non–Latin–speaking peoples because of the unintelligible sounds of their languages. The Arabs took up the designation *barbar*, a term with the double meaning of incomprehensible speech and "barbarian" behavior. Historically, Berbers referred to themselves by tribal or regional names, although there is some evidence that a version of the more general term *Imazighen* was used in the Roman era. Today *Imazighen* connotes a pan-regional sense of Berber identity and is generally interpreted to mean "free men."

Since the 1980s, Amazigh cultural associations in Algeria, Morocco, France, and elsewhere have advocated for increased recognition of the Berber language and culture by the states of North Africa. As a result, the Moroccan and Algerian governments have taken significant steps in that direction, although many activists would

Three-bodied ceramic vessel with spout, from Kabylia, Algeria, decorated in mineral pigments and natural resin glaze. The triangular and diamond-shaped motifs on pottery vessels from Kabylia are often given names—fibulas, scorpions, soldiers—indicating that they offer protective power. This piece is one of the oldest examples of Berber art in the Peabody Museum. Given by the Boston Museum of Fine Arts in 1904. PM 04-22-50/64057 (H 24.8 × W 19.1 × D 16.8 cm). T4833.3. Hillel S. Burger, photographer.

argue that there is still a long way to go. The government of Algeria declared Tamazight a national language in 2002, and it is being taught in some schools both there and in Morocco. An official body devoted to Berber studies, the Royal Institute for Amazigh Culture, was formed in Morocco in 2001. A similar institution, the Algerian Academy of the Amazigh Language, has recently been established as well.

When referring to the transnational Berber identity that has emerged from this growing social movement, some activists prefer the term *Amazigh*, arguing that *Berber* still carries the derogatory meanings connected with the Latin *barbarus* and the English "barbarian." Use of *Amazigh* varies; Moroccan activists, for example, employ it more commonly than Algerian activists do. Most Berbers continue to refer to themselves in other terms that denote regional and linguistic identifications. People from the three regions discussed in this book might call themselves Leqbayel (Kabyles), Irifiyen (Riffians), or Kel Ahaggar (people of the Ahaggar region) rather than Berbers or Imazighen. They might also use even more locally specific names associated with tribal groups, such as At Yenni.[6] In this book I use *Amazigh* and *Imazighen* interchangeably with *Berber(s)* to refer to phenomena that transcend specific regional identities. I use local terms to specify the arts or language of a particular region.

That most Imazighen continue to identify themselves using regionally specific terms underscores the fact that despite many historical and linguistic commonalities, Berber speakers are diverse in both appearance and way of life. The three Berber regions of North Africa represented in the Peabody Museum's collections exemplify some of this diversity. The Berbers of Kabylia and the Rif, the mountainous, northernmost Berber-speaking regions, are organized into small, settled agricultural communities of extended patrilineal family groups governed by tribal councils. Villagers in these regions traditionally practiced herding and subsistence agriculture, supplemented today by money sent home by family members working outside the villages.

In contrast to these settled agriculturalists in the north, the Tuareg, the southernmost Berber-speaking people, are nomadic pastoralists who migrate over long distances with their herds of camels and goats. Much has changed as Tuareg communities have increasingly settled in towns and villages since Algerian independence in 1962, but traditionally these Berber speakers had a highly stratified society, with a camel-riding noble class and a goat-herding vassal class. In another striking contrast with northern Berber societies, the Tuareg follow a matrilineal descent pattern, in which each societal subgroup traces its origin back to a single female ancestor. Alongside these two broad social configurations, a third type of society is found among Berber speakers living between the mountains and the desert. These groups, including the Berbers of the foothills of the High Atlas Mountains in Morocco, practice settled agriculture for some months of the year but at other times migrate with their flocks within fixed territories.

This brief description of Berber societies is of course very general, and the social structures associated with "traditional" Berber society have changed over time. Today many Berber regions support larger towns and cities where these patterns of rural life do not apply. In addition, many people of Berber origin have migrated to the cities of North Africa, Europe, and North America. Even as the Peabody Museum's collections were being constituted in the late nineteenth and early twentieth centuries, Berber societies were undergoing significant changes that would leave lasting imprints on their ways of life and material culture.

The Peabody Museum acquired its first collection of Amazigh art in 1904, in an accession from the Boston Museum of Fine Arts that included nine painted pottery pieces from Algeria. These pieces and other early collections from North Africa came from prominent Bostonians who donated pottery, jewelry, and textiles they had acquired during their travels abroad. As both the Peabody Museum and Harvard's

Department of Anthropology broadened the scope of their research in the twentieth century, the museum's collections grew through the efforts of professional anthropologists who conducted studies in Morocco and Algeria. Two Harvard anthropologists, Carleton S. Coon (1904–1981, Harvard Ph.D. 1928) and Lloyd Cabot Briggs (1909–1975, Harvard Ph.D. 1952), were instrumental in shaping the Peabody's collections from North Africa. Although both were interested in Berber-speaking peoples in general, they focused their research and collecting on two regions—Coon on the Rif in northern Morocco and Briggs on the Tuareg regions of the Algerian Sahara.

Coon and Briggs brought back to the Peabody collections of significant depth from their two key regions. Other Berber parts of Algeria and large swaths of Berber-speaking Morocco are only barely represented in the museum's collections. The collectors who donated objects to the Peabody were inspired by different motivations; their efforts were not part of a larger project to document Berber life across North Africa. The result is not a complete or consistent collection of "Amazigh art."[7] But by examining individual pieces, we can gain insights into both the remarkable diversity of Berber material culture and a common aesthetic that often transcends differences of geography and social life.

The Berber arts have coexisted with other North African forms of material expression since pre-Islamic times. Phoenicians, Romans, and Byzantines all left behind vestiges of visual culture in the form of statuary and mosaics depicting daily life. After the coming of Islam, arts such as tilework, ceramics, metalwork, and silk weaving developed in the cities of North Africa. In contrast, the Amazigh tradition is based not on representational art or on these more urban art forms but on the embellishment of everyday objects. Living in the harsh world of North Africa's mountains and deserts, most Imazighen at the time the Peabody's collections were formed owned few material possessions. Pottery, textiles, wooden implements, and leather goods all filled the needs of daily life. Yet artisans often designed and decorated even the most utilitarian objects just as carefully as they did more ornamental pieces such as jewelry and weaponry.

The embellishments on these objects partake of a shared language of geometric motifs still found across the Berber-speaking world. Geometric designs appear on textiles, pottery, jewelry, and leatherwork. They are incorporated into architecture and painted on interior walls, and they are inscribed on the body in the form of tattoos. The rich array of symbols connects these everyday objects to more abstract traditions and beliefs. Some motifs are inspired by the Berber alphabet, Tifinagh (pl. 1). The Tifinagh script is thought to have symbolic power and is used in protective inscriptions. Other symbols have names given to them by their creators—carding comb, scorpion, serpent, honeycomb, water, fields—evidence that even the simplest motifs are tied to a symbolic realm. These names vary from place to place and over time, so attaching meaning to specific symbols must be done with caution.[8] The names suggest, however, that many decorative motifs are used as protective symbols or to represent fertility and abundance. Berber women's arts and dress often incorporate colors and motifs associated with fertility, drawing a connection between women's creative powers, reproduction, and the fertility of the land.[9]

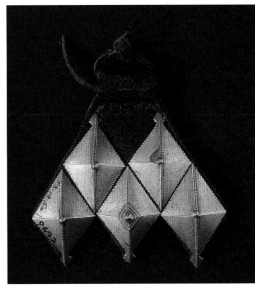

Leather and silver alloy pendant. Of a type worn by Tuareg women in the Algerian Sahara, this pendant is an abstract version of a hand, a common protective symbol. Its name, *khomessa*, comes from the Arabic word for "five." Collected by Lloyd Cabot Briggs in 1953. PM 53-14-50/9642 (H 5.8 × W 5.8 × D 0.8 cm). T4991.1. Hillel S. Burger, photographer.

Many of the motifs found in Amazigh art are symbols used for protection, especially against the "evil eye" and other malevolent forces.[10] Fear of the evil eye springs from an ancient belief found all around the Mediterranean basin—the idea that envy is a dangerous force. An ill-natured or covetous look, whether intentional or not, can be destructive, so it is necessary to protect oneself and one's belongings. One means of protection is to keep precious objects out of sight, preventing the evil gaze from falling on them in the first place. People who are especially vulnerable to the evil eye, such as brides and newborn babies, may be hidden behind veils or wrapped in cloths, respectively, to protect them from the gazes of others. Another means of protection is to thwart the harmful glance by directing it instead toward a less desirable, even repulsive object that will disgust and repel it. A blackened pot placed outside a newly constructed house and a hedgehog jaw tied to the fringe of a leather bag (pl. 16) are examples of this method of protection.

Still another means of protecting oneself and one's belongings is to make ample use of symbols considered effective at turning aside the evil eye. One of the symbols most frequently used as an antidote to the evil eye is the hand. Across North Africa and the Middle East, artisans incorporate hand-shaped symbols into jewelry, pendants, plaques, and even stickers hung as protection in houses, offices, shops, and cars. The symbolic hand appears in Amazigh art as both a literal hand shape (pl. 2) and in more abstract versions that incorporate elements of five. The leather and silver pendant from the Algerian Sahara shown on page 11, an everyday item of jewelry worn by Tuareg women, is called a *khomessa*, from the Arabic word for "five" (*khamsa*). Its five silver diamond shapes are said to represent the five fingers of the hand. Symbols consisting of hands, elements of five, or sets of five lines that may represent fingers can also be found painted on pottery and woven into textiles. The Finnish scholar Edward Westermarck, writing about practices common in Morocco in the early twentieth century, described a motif often found on the upper parts of painted Riffian pottery vessels as representing pairs of outstretched hands. He mentioned other motifs incorporating elements of five, such as checkerboards and rosettes, as additional protective symbols.[11]

In many parts of the Berber-speaking world, triangular shapes are also considered effective against the evil eye. Kabyle pottery designs make use of many different triangular motifs. Some of these designs are called "fibulas," a reference to the brooches that were once integral parts of Kabyle women's dress (see pl. 10). Both the triangular form and the pointed pin of the brooch are seen as effective weapons against the evil eye. The Tuareg, too, consider the triangle a protective form, and Tuareg artisans make frequent use of the triangle as a decorative motif (pl. 3). The triangular shapes used in Tuareg jewelry may also serve as amulets, holding verses from the Qur'an or other protective phrases written on pieces of paper hidden inside the decorated silver case.[12]

Lozenge or diamond patterns, sometimes called "eyes," also appear on textiles and pottery from the Berber world. Perhaps the most striking example of the "good" eye, used as protection against its evil counterpart, is found in the woven cloaks made by the Ait Ouaouzguite Berbers of the Siroua Mountain region, between the High and Anti-Atlas Mountains of Morocco (pl. 4). The large red eye emblazoned on the back

Milk pot from the Rif, Morocco. Symbols incorporating elements of five, like those in the checker-board and rosette patterns seen here, are found frequently on pottery and textiles from the Berber-speaking world. These symbols, as well as the outstretched "hands" on the upper part of the vessel, may have served a protective function. Collected by Carleton Coon in 1926. PM 27-37-50/B4359 (H 15 × W 20.8 × D 17 cm). 98520057. Mark Craig, photographer.

of each cloak is often supplemented by smaller lozenge shapes and other motifs decorating the garment. These may serve a protective purpose as well, and lozenges are also frequently interpreted as fertility symbols.

Although the protective purposes of symbols such as the hand and eye are clear, the meanings of other symbols in the Amazigh design vocabulary are less evident (pl. 5). In creating painted pots, woven textiles, or embroidered leather bags, artisans from across the Berber-speaking world draw on a symbolic vocabulary that is both regionally specific and part of a larger symbolic universe. Like the Berber language, which is spoken in regional varieties, so the symbolic language manifests itself in different forms—the abstract hand of a Tuareg pendant is very different from that on a painted Riffian pot. Often regional design traditions vary to the extent that a woven textile or painted pottery piece can be ascribed to a specific subregion, village, or tribe on the basis of the artisan's use of color and choice of motifs. The symbolic design vocabulary of Amazigh arts is associated primarily with women's work—patterned textiles and painted pottery in the north, embroidered leatherwork in the south. But Berber men, too, manufacture objects that are rich in symbolism (pl. 6). Working with local resources and within an aesthetic that spans North Africa, Berber artisans create beautiful objects that reflect many aspects of their worldview and beliefs.

Most of the objects in the Peabody Museum's collection of Amazigh art were created and collected between the late nineteenth and the mid-twentieth century. During this period most of the states of North Africa came under colonial rule, making it a time of profound social and economic changes that greatly altered the material culture of the Berber-speaking world. In many regions, textiles and pottery used daily were replaced by factory-produced fabrics and metal or plastic containers. Traditional art objects also became part of a new global market as tourists and colonial administrators took interest in their aesthetic and commercial value.

This is not to say that Berber arts had remained static before the coming of European goods and markets. Berbers had been involved since ancient times in trade relations that affected their material culture. Nevertheless, the modern travelers and anthropologists who collected these objects saw them as material evidence of a culture that was changing rapidly and perhaps even on its way to disappearing. Their assumption was wrong: Berber language, material culture, and cultural traditions continue to thrive across North Africa. But the economic and social conditions of the colonial period did have an important influence that becomes evident when we take a closer look at the history and culture behind the objects that make up the Peabody Museum's collection of Amazigh art.

Kabyle family, late nineteenth century. Among other jewelry, the women and girls wear head ornaments like that shown in plate 11. Photograph probably purchased in Algeria in 1902; donated by the heirs of Charles P. Bowditch in 1946. PM 46-40-50/13125.

*As the country of Kabylia is justly considered to be the finest
part of Algeria, no tourist can reasonably omit from his
excursion list this magnificent mountainous region, termed
by many the "Switzerland of Africa."*
—Joseph C. Hyam, *The Illustrated Guide to Algiers,* 1908

Touring Kabylia

THE COLLECTION OF POTTERY, TEXTILES, AND JEWELRY from Kabylia
housed at the Peabody Museum is a small but significant group dating to the late
nineteenth and very early twentieth centuries. Most of the pieces, part of a growing
commerce between Kabyle artisans and foreign travelers, were collected between
1870 and 1905 by Bostonians enjoying leisure trips to Algeria. These decades saw
great economic and social changes in the region as the French established their control and opened Kabylia to new markets, which led to important changes in the material culture of the time. Pottery vessels used to carry and store water and oil were
replaced in some places by imported metal and, later, plastic containers. Dresses
made of prefabricated cotton cloth came into fashion while handwoven woolen garments continued to be worn mostly by older women. Changing styles and economic
conditions also brought changes to Kabyle women's enameled silver jewelry.

Even as local tastes and demands changed, Kabyle artisans found new markets for
their products among tourists and colonial administrators in Kabylia and the cities of

Algeria. The Peabody's objects from Kabylia were gathered by travelers with a passing interest in Algeria and Kabyle culture, not by anthropologists intent on studying the region in depth. The collection reflects this history, telling us much about the travelers' tastes and interests. It also shows the ingenuity of Kabyle artisans as they developed products for new markets and changing tastes.

The region known as Kabylia extends along the mountainous coast of eastern Algeria and is dominated by two major mountain ranges, the Djurdjura in the west and the Babor in the east. The western part of the region, known as Greater Kabylia under the French, has as its main administrative center the city of Tizi Ouzou. The eastern part, Lesser Kabylia, extends south from the coast between the cities of Bejaïa (called Bougie under the French) and Jijel. In both areas Taqbaylit, the local variety of Berber, is most people's first language, although most Kabyles speak Arabic (the language of public education since Algerian independence) or French as well. The terms *Kabylia* and *Kabyle*, derived from the Arabic word for "tribe" (*qabīla*), were coined by Europeans in the eighteenth century in reference to these mountainous areas and the tribesmen who inhabited them.

Europeans perceived the Kabyles as rugged mountaineers, fiercely independent and living in almost complete isolation from outside influence. Colonial-era scholarship on the region reinforced such stereotypes by constructing an image of the Kabyles as living in self-sufficient miniature democracies. At the time of French colonization, herding and subsistence agriculture filled many of people's daily needs in the region. But the Kabyles had also been connected to one another and to people in other regions through complex networks of exchange long before the arrival of the French. The French perception of the democratic or egalitarian nature of Kabyle society was also exaggerated. Although the tribal councils that governed Kabyle villages generally did include male representatives from all the families of the community, more recent scholarship has shown that inequalities in wealth and power existed nonetheless.[13]

The precolonial social and economic organization of Kabylia was severely disrupted by French occupation and settlement of the region, which was one of the last to fall under French control. Although the French took Algiers in 1830, they did not consider

Kabylia "pacified" until 1857, when a large fortification was built southeast of Tizi Ouzou at what is today Larbaa Naït Irathen, called Fort National under the French. The inhabitants of Kabylia continued to resist French occupation even after that date, battling soldiers and settlers for another ten years. The last major revolt against French domination, in 1871, brought harsh expropriations of Kabyle land in retaliation. The colonial government used confiscated land to establish French-owned farms and villages throughout the region. Kabyle farmers, meanwhile, were left to eke out livings on increasingly smaller plots. Many were forced to leave their natal villages to look for seasonal work on European settlers' farms or in the cities of Algeria. By World War I this exodus had led Kabyle men as far as France, where they worked in factories or as agricultural laborers, sending remittances home to support their families in Kabylia.

It was among these workers in the cities of France, many of them Kabyles, that the movement for Algerian independence first began to take hold. Kabyle political leaders were prominent in the nationalist movement and during the war for independence (1954–1962), linking their political activism for the end of French rule to an emphasis on the plurality of Algerian national identity. Their efforts were silenced, however, as both the nationalist movement and post-independence governments emphasized a unified, Arabo-Islamic cultural identity rather than taking a pluralist view that might have incorporated a Berber element. The Arabization of the education system and the media and the new Algerian state's reluctance to support the study of Berber language and culture led to increasing frustration among Kabyle intellectuals. In 1980, in response to the cancellation of a lecture on Kabyle poetry at the University of Tizi Ouzou, Kabyles demonstrated across the region. Historians now see this period, called the Berber Spring, as marking the emergence of a truly widespread Berber political consciousness.[14]

Kabyle activists in both Kabylia and France have played important roles in the now transnational Amazigh rights movement, demanding further recognition of the Berber language and culture by the states of North Africa. A year-long boycott of schools in Kabylia in 1994–1995 led to the beginning of Tamazight instruction in some Algerian public schools. Following a year of violent demonstrations known as

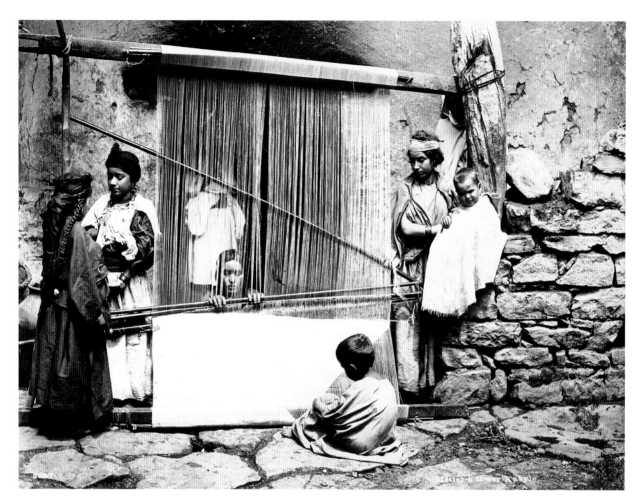

Kabyle women and children working at a loom. Photograph probably purchased in Algeria in 1902; donated by the heirs of Charles P. Bowditch in 1946. PM 46-40-50/13124.

the Black Spring, which began in April 2001, the Algerian constitution was revised to include Tamazight as a national (though not official) language. Kabylia also found itself caught up in the Algerian civil war of 1991–2002, a conflict between armed Islamist groups and state security forces in which more than 150,000 people, mostly civilians, died. Berber activists, many of whom oppose the Algerian state but advocate for a secular and democratic Algeria, have been targeted by the Islamist groups. The official end of the civil war in 2002 did not mean a complete cessation of hostilities, but many people hoped the relative calm would allow for the return of Kabyles who went into exile during the war.

The art from Kabylia at the Peabody Museum was collected during the period of French control of the region. Prominent Bostonians making pleasure trips to Algeria purchased pottery, textiles, and jewelry as souvenirs of an excursion abroad and often kept the pieces for many years. Only later did these objects reach the Peabody through donations made late in the collectors' lives or by their heirs. Kabyle pieces never attained the "art object" status afforded to masks and statuary from sub–Saharan Africa; they were purchased by tourists as "curiosities" or decorative items. Although it is difficult to trace exactly where or why specific collectors purchased the objects they did or what they did with them upon their return, it is likely that many of these pieces decorated their owners' homes before being donated to the museum.

During their travels in Algeria, these Bostonians joined other foreign visitors drawn to the warm climate and what they perceived as the exotic ambience of the southern Mediterranean. Tourists had begun to visit Algeria in significant numbers after regular passenger ferry service was established between Marseilles and Algiers in the 1860s. At first most tourists stayed in Algiers, relaxing in the sunny weather, touring the scenic "native" parts of the city, and enjoying the luxuries provided by French hotels and restaurants. Travel guides touted the city as "the best winter residence within easy range of England," and it found popularity with many European and even American travelers.[15]

By the 1870s trips to the interior of the country had become staples of tourists' sojourns in Algeria. Kabylia, with its dramatic scenery and picturesque mountaintop villages within easy reach of Algiers, became a main destination for tourists who wanted to see more than just the capital city. Visitors traveled by carriage, and later by train, from Algiers to Tizi Ouzou. From there they could continue by carriage southeast to Fort National, which had by this time expanded to become a fortified French town with spectacular views of the Djurdjura Mountains. Tourists could also organize excursions, on their own or with the aid of companies such as Thomas Cook and Sons, from Tizi Ouzou and Fort National into Kabyle villages.

Travelers looking for lasting souvenirs could purchase Kabyle art in Algiers as well as in markets in Kabylia and other parts of the country. Three types of Kabyle crafts-manship—pottery, jewelry, and textiles—were especially popular. In Algiers these could be found in large shops offering wide ranges of products—embroidery, carpets, pottery, jewelry, antiquities—from all over Algeria, as well as from Morocco, Tunisia, Egypt, and even Turkey, India, and Persia. Visitors could also purchase souvenirs in Kabylia at weekly markets or from individuals. Guidebooks of the time mentioned certain villages known for their artisanal production and gave practical hints about where to obtain the best souvenirs:

> The native market, held on Saturday morning near the railway station [in Tizi Ouzou], is worth noticing; the Kabyles come there in overwhelming numbers, bringing their asses, cows, mules, honey, oil, leather, corn and all sorts of wares. The Kabyle pottery is sold very cheap, and can be utilised for ornamenting brackets, &c. The gandouras and foutas [woven garments] . . . make also very good souvenirs of the country. The Kabyle necklaces and earrings of white metal are very curious; they are sold for a few francs, but the largest assortment of these is to be found at the villages of the Beni Enni [At Yenni], near Fort National, where they are manufactured.[16]

The Kabyle objects in the Peabody Museum are similar to those described in the guidebook just quoted—decorative pottery, woven garments, and silver jewelry.[17] Some of these pieces may have been made specifically for the foreign trade; others were more likely older pieces sold to travelers or merchants by families in need of extra income.

The oldest pieces of Berber craftsmanship at the Peabody are a group of painted pottery vessels from Kabylia. The Peabody acquired them through an accession from the Boston Museum of Fine Arts, whose trustees had decided that this pottery and some other objects from around the world were "no longer within [the museum's] proper scope, their interest being ethnological rather than artistic."[18] The pottery had been donated to the Museum of Fine Arts in two groups. In 1878, Miss A. M. Towne donated four pieces of Kabyle pottery "painted by the women of the tribes inhabiting the mountains of Algeria." In 1890, eighteen pieces of "Kabyle and Moorish" pottery came to the museum from Thornton K. Lothrop.[19] Until they were deposited in the Peabody Museum in 1904, these pieces were displayed in a room devoted to pottery and porcelain from around the world in the original Museum of Fine Arts building in Copley Square.

Thornton Kirkland Lothrop (1830–1913) was a prominent New England lawyer who had served as assistant United States district attorney during the Civil War.[20] He probably purchased his "Kabyle and Moorish" pottery during a trip he made to Algeria sometime between 1878 and 1890; an 1878 edition of *Murray's Handbook for Travelers in Algeria and Tunis* with his name inscribed on the title page is in the collections of Harvard's Widener Library. Lothrop was a trustee of the Boston Museum of Fine Arts and may have purchased these examples of Algerian pottery expressly to donate them to the museum.

In 1942, more than fifty years after Lothrop's original donation, his daughter gave three more pieces of painted Kabyle pottery to the Peabody Museum (pl. 7). According to museum records, she acquired them in the mountains near Algiers in 1882, perhaps having accompanied her father on his trip. Her husband, Dr. Algernon Coolidge, also donated Kabyle pottery to the Peabody Museum (see illustration on p. 28). He most likely purchased these pieces while on a separate trip to Algeria and Egypt in 1891. Dr. and Mrs. Coolidge acquired their Kabyle pots while still quite young, before they were married, but kept them as souvenirs of their visits to Algeria until late in life.[21]

Other objects in the Peabody collections acquired by travelers to Algeria include three intricately woven textiles donated by the daughters of Mrs. R. M. Appleton in 1936 and 1941 (pl. 9). One of Mrs. Appleton's daughters was Madeleine Kidder, the wife of Harvard–trained archaeologist Alfred Vincent Kidder. According to

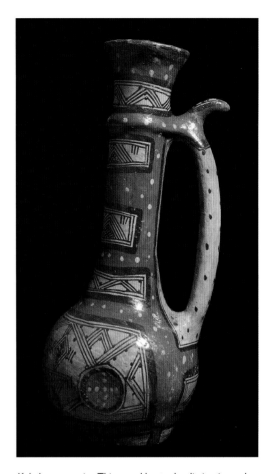

Kabyle pottery jar. This vessel bears the distinctive red, black, and yellow designs of the At Aïssi, a Kabyle tribe whose pottery was especially popular among tourists. It was purchased in Algeria before 1890 and donated to the Boston Museum of Fine Arts, which gave it to the Peabody in 1904. PM 04-22-50/64055 (H 34.3 × W 13.6 × D 14 cm). 98520051. Mark Craig, photographer.

Kabyle women carrying water jars from a spring, late nineteenth century. Photograph probably purchased in Algeria in 1902; donated by the heirs of Charles P. Bowditch in 1946. PM 2004.29.11115.

museum records, Mrs. Appleton purchased these pieces in Algiers in 1904.[22] They are beautiful examples of an older type of woman's handwoven costume. If they were purchased in Algiers, then it was probably through a merchant who dealt in older Kabyle pieces along with objects from other regions.

The largest collection of Kabyle art at the Peabody arrived in 1946 as a donation from the heirs of Charles Pickering Bowditch (pls. 10, 11). This accession included painted pottery, enameled silver jewelry, and a collection of professionally made photographs depicting scenes of daily life in Kabylia.[23] Charles P. Bowditch (1842–1921) was best known for his studies of Mayan writing systems and for his work as a Boston businessman and benefactor to many organizations, including the Peabody Museum. After a trip to Mexico in 1888 Bowditch became intensely interested in Central American archaeology and eventually became a leading figure in the field. He sponsored the Peabody Museum's early expeditions to Central America and helped foster the careers of many archaeologists working in the region. The donations and other support he gave to the museum during his lifetime contributed to the formation of significant research collections and the establishment of Harvard as a leading institution in Central American archaeology.

Bowditch and his family were frequent travelers, and they most likely acquired the objects in the Peabody collections during a trip to Algeria in 1902.[24] The Bowditches made at least two trips to North Africa. The first, in March 1898, was a two-week, whirlwind tour of the country during which Charles Bowditch, his wife, Cornelia, and their daughter Katherine visited Algiers, Bejaïa, Sétif, Biskra, Batna, and Constantine before continuing to Tunis. The second trip, from December 1901 to March 1902, took a more leisurely pace, although not by intention. Mr. and Mrs. Bowditch, their daughter Cora (Cornelia), and niece Fanny arrived in Algiers in early December 1901. About two weeks into their stay, during an excursion to some Roman ruins, they suffered a carriage accident. Mrs. Bowditch's arm was broken, and the family had to prolong its stay in Algiers while she recuperated. The travelers eventually spent two weeks at the thermal baths of Hammam Righa, southwest of Algiers, before retracing their route of four years earlier, starting in Bejaïa and ending in Tunis.

During the family's stay of almost two months in the capital city, Charles Bowditch made a few excursions to Fort National and into the surrounding villages. He described the first of these trips in a long letter to his daughter Lucy, dated January 10, 1902. He and his traveling companion rode mules along a precipitous mountain path to arrive at the villages of the At Yenni, where Bowditch made some purchases from the locally renowned jewelers. His descriptions capture the attractions of the region for visitors of his time—the majestic scenery and the picturesque villages, which seemed to evoke ancient times:

Generally the side hills were covered with green and as we came out on the point of some ridge the view would stretch itself out on both hands and the long green valley would be seen with a dozen sharp ridges jutting out on either side and the stream below cutting a circuitous path amongst them. And on many of the very tops of the ridges you can see the Kabyle villages perched with their white walls and tile or thatched roofs like eagles' eyries. . . . And in places the path would be filled by old women and girls carrying baskets on their shoulders and backs or great jars (some of which I will show you if they don't get all broken to pieces) for water. . . . it would be very easy to pick out Rebekah at the well and other Biblical characters.[25]

Much of the jewelry in the Peabody collections bears the enameled designs and coral work associated with jewelers of the villages Bowditch visited. Other pieces might have been purchased by his family members in Algiers or elsewhere. His daughter Cornelia wrote to her sisters of frequent shopping trips, saying that "it is very difficult to know how much to buy here. I feel as if I didn't buy some of this jewelry which is so fascinating that I shall be sorry."[26] The Bowditch collection from Algeria was not donated to the Peabody Museum until 1946, shortly after Cornelia, who never married and continued to live in the family home in Jamaica Plain after her parents' deaths, had passed away. Perhaps she kept these items as mementos of their journey together.

Other objects from Kabylia in the Peabody Museum had life histories similar to those of the Bowditch family donations—they were pieces purchased by visitors to Algeria at the end of the nineteenth century as interesting things to show family and friends upon their return. Many of the objects did not arrive at the museum until the 1930s or 1940s, as gifts from the heirs of the original collectors. This collection of Kabyle art offers insights into the tastes and interests of turn-of-the-century travelers in the region. It also reveals some of the changes taking place in Kabyle arts in response to the social and economic changes intensified by French colonialism and the establishment of tourism in Algeria.

In an exhaustive work on Kabyle society in the early years of French occupation, Adolphe Hanoteau and Aristide Letourneux inventoried the types of industries found in Kabylia.[27] These included the manufacture of olive oil, soap, gunpowder, and wax for sale both within and without the region. The writers also discussed domestic industries such as pottery making and textile weaving and more specialized products such as weaponry and jewelry. Making pottery and weaving were women's domains, practiced throughout the countryside as mothers passed their skills down to their daughters. Craftswomen rarely marketed their products; they made objects mostly to meet their families' needs or acquired pottery from a skilled neighbor in return for grain or some other item of barter. Forging metal for weapons and making silver jewelry were male occupations, centralized in certain villages known for their expert craftsmen. Artisans made these products on demand or sold them at regional markets alongside other products made primarily by men—woven linen cloth, tanned skins, and agricultural implements.

Kabyle pottery making was one industry that underwent significant changes during the colonial period.[28] Kabyle women made fired pottery vessels to carry and store water, milk, and oil (pl. 7); as cooking pots, couscous steamers, and oil strainers; and as serving plates and drinking cups. They used local clays and formed their vessels without the aid of a potter's wheel. They painted the pots with mineral pigments and then fired them in the open air. Rubbing the vessel with pine resin after it was fired created the distinctive yellow color of some Kabyle pottery. Painted patterns

Circular brooch (*tabzimt* or *tafzimt*) from Kabylia, made of silver alloy, enamel, and imitation coral. Such brooches may be worn on the forehead or the chest, and in some Berber areas they signal that the owner has given birth to a son. The intricate enamel and coral designs are associated with jewelers of the At Yenni, and the piece was probably purchased by Charles Bowditch during a trip to the At Yenni villages in 1902. Donated by the heirs of Charles P. Bowditch in 1946. PM 46-40-50/5969 (H 7.5 × W 10.5 × D 0.3 cm). 98520085. Mark Craig, photographer.

Large water jar from Kabylia, Algeria. Vessels painted in a solid red pigment accented by black decoration are often associated with the village of Taourirt Amokrane, which was accessible to tourists from the French administrative center, Fort National (now Larbaa Naït Irathen). This piece was collected around 1891 by Dr. Algernon Coolidge, who may have purchased it in Taourirt Amokrane. PM 31-27-50/B5084 (H 60.4 × W 36.9 × D 30.2 cm). 98520066. Mark Craig, photographer.

varied from place to place, each craftswoman developing her own designs from the motifs commonly used around her. The large red water jar illustrated on page 28, for example, was typical of work from the village of Taourirt Amokrane. The red, black, and yellow designs of the vessel shown on page 23 were associated with the villages of the At Aïssi, and it was this type of pottery that became particularly popular among foreign visitors to the region.

Even at the time of their research in 1868, Hanoteau and Letourneux characterized At Aïssi pottery as the kind "one finds for sale in Algiers, and is sought after by the French public as objects of curiosity."[29] They described new forms being produced for sale in markets, based on European vases and even Christian chalices. In 1911 French ethnographer Arnold van Gennep carried out an extensive survey of Kabyle pottery production. He found that by this time the At Aïssi were generally using imported metal containers for their household needs, but they continued to make painted pottery to meet the demands of European tourists. This type of pottery makes up the majority of the Peabody Museum's collections from Kabylia (pl. 8). Van Gennep's observations applied mainly to one type of Kabyle pottery; throughout the colonial period pottery continued to be made for domestic use in many parts of Kabylia. The industry continues to some extent today, although now painted pottery is used more often for decoration than for functional purposes.

In the late nineteenth century, similar changes took place in other realms of Kabyle artistic production as well. Prefabricated cotton cloth became widely available and affordable, so women did not have to spend as much time weaving for their families' clothing.[30] Women began wearing the *taqendurt*, a colorful cotton dress with an embroidered front panel, instead of the older woven garments, the *axellal* and the *ddil* (pl. 9). These older garments, made of handwoven woolen cloth, were worn draped around the body and fastened at the shoulders with large triangular brooches (pl. 10). As cotton dresses replaced the *axellal* and the *ddil*, older jewelry forms became less necessary.[31] Some of the larger pieces worn by Kabyle women went out of fashion, although many were reworked into new forms that continue to be made and worn today (pl. 11). Kabyle jewelers adapted their production to appeal to changing local tastes and often sold older pieces to foreigners looking for souvenirs. French settlement of land formerly farmed by Kabyles and the displacement of farmers into the cash economy meant that many families had to look for new sources of income. Sale of their traditional handicrafts or older pieces of clothing and jewelry was one means for people to provide for their families.

The painted pottery, handwoven textiles, and silver jewelry in the Peabody Museum collections were part of a burgeoning commerce between Kabyle artisans and foreign travelers. As local fashions and economic conditions changed, traditional arts took on new forms and found new markets. This commercialization did not detract from the objects' beauty or from the skill of the Kabyle craftspeople who produced them. New markets gave rise to new forms of expression, but those forms were founded in a long tradition of rich and symbolic design that flourishes to this day.

Mohammed Limnibhy and some of Carleton Coon's other companions in the Rif. Left to right: al-Sayyid Jilali, Sheikh Si Moh wild el-Hajj Bukkeish, Mohammed Limnibhy, and Akshar. Photograph taken between 1926 and 1931. Carleton S. Coon Papers (Box 16), National Anthropological Archives, Smithsonian Institution.

We had lived briefly among a friendly people who were still free, and who, with Midboh's [the French-appointed sheikh's] help, had been allowed to meet a new and more compatible kind of Christians.
—Carleton S. Coon, *Adventures and Discoveries,* 1981

HARVARD IN THE RIF

IN CONTRAST TO THE OBJECTS FROM KABYLIA, purchased by tourists during brief visits to Algeria, the Peabody Museum's collections from the Rif were gathered by a Harvard-trained anthropologist carrying out research in the region. Carleton S. Coon did his doctoral research in Morocco, where he gathered physical and sociological data about the inhabitants of the Rif and other regions. The pottery, leatherwork, clothing, and other materials Coon collected and donated to the Peabody Museum were not simply souvenirs of a trip abroad but were meant to represent aspects of daily life and Riffian craftsmanship. Coon purchased most of his pieces at rural and urban markets and received some as gifts from friends and informants. Unlike Lloyd Cabot Briggs, whose collection of Tuareg art features in the next chapter, Coon was not engaged in a long-term collecting project in the Rif, and his acquisitions did not make up a systematic or thorough catalogue of Riffian arts. His research interests were only tangentially connected to material culture. Nevertheless, the examples of early-twentieth-century Riffian craftsmanship now housed at the Peabody Museum give us a glimpse of life in northern Morocco during an important time, when the region was first coming under European control. They offer insights into some of the changes then taking place in material culture, and they highlight a distinctive local design tradition within the larger context of Amazigh arts.

The Rif Mountains stretch along the Mediterranean coast of Morocco between the cities of Tetouan and Nador, extending south almost to Taza and Fes. The entire region is often referred to as the Rif (pronounced *reef*); in Berber it is called Arīf, and in Arabic, al-Rīf, which also means "countryside." Culturally the Rif is divided into a western portion, inhabited by Arabic speakers, and an eastern portion, where the local variety of Berber, called Tarifit, is spoken. Within the eastern area, south of Al Hoceima and east of Targuist, lies what Coon and later anthropologists referred to as the central Rif.[32] Although the region is dominated by the Rif Mountains, it also encompasses fertile plains south and east of the coastal peaks. At the time of Coon's research, most inhabitants of the Rif were settled agriculturalists, though some of the eastern Riffian tribes migrated seasonally with their flocks. Both Coon and David Hart, an American anthropologist who worked in the region somewhat later than Coon, described the central Rif of the early to mid-twentieth century as divided into tribal areas, each consisting of several scattered villages and market centers governed by tribal councils.

Carleton Coon first visited the Rif in September 1926. The Riffian tribes had only recently surrendered to French and Spanish forces whom they had been fighting fiercely for the previous five years. Spain had established a sphere of influence in northern Morocco and along the Saharan coast in 1904, and when France declared a protectorate in the rest of the country in 1912, Spain claimed these regions for itself. The Riffian tribes strongly resisted the imposition of foreign rule by either country. In 1921 Spanish troops attempted to occupy a large part of the Rif but were pushed back by a well-organized resistance movement under the leadership of the legendary Riffian warrior Muhammad Ibn ʿAbd al-Karim al-Khattabi. Abd el-Krim, as he was generally known, declared an independent Riffian Republic in the central Rif in 1921, but eventually France and Spain united to defeat his armies with overwhelming force. Abd el-Krim surrendered in May 1926, although armed resistance to the European presence continued in some areas for more than another year. The Rif remained part of the Spanish protectorate until Moroccan independence in 1956.

Following independence and the reunification of the former French and Spanish zones under King Muhammad V, the Rif found itself economically and politically marginalized, a situation that led to an uprising in 1958–1959 that was put down harshly by the Moroccan army. The region continues to suffer from economic hardship and, like Kabylia, has a long history of emigration. In the late nineteenth and early twentieth centuries, oversettlement of Riffian land generated a steady flow of migrant laborers from the Rif to Algeria, where Riffians worked on newly established French farms. In the 1960s Europe became the destination for Riffian labor migrants, and people of Riffian origin continue to form a substantial portion of the immigrant population in certain countries, especially the Netherlands.

Today agriculture, including an important industry devoted to the illegal cultivation of cannabis, and remittances from family members working abroad are the main sources of income in rural areas. In cities such as Nador and Al Hoceima, Riffians play important roles in trade, both licit and illicit, between Europe and North Africa.[33] Tarifit is the first language in the Rif, although Riffians, like most other Berber speakers, are likely to speak Arabic or another language as well. For many migrants, Dutch has supplanted Spanish or French as an acquired European language. Riffians have also played active roles in the transnational Amazigh rights movement, and Amazigh associations in the cities and the countryside advocate for increased recognition of the Berber language and culture as well as for economic development.

Carleton Stevens Coon was a self-described adventurer, and it was the Riffians' reputation for independence and resistance that first drew him to the region. Coon was born in 1904 in Wakefield, Massachusetts. He graduated in 1925 from Harvard College, where he studied anthropology with Earnest A. Hooton, the department's prominent physical anthropologist. He went on to write his Ph.D. dissertation under Hooton's direction and carried out research for it during four trips to Morocco between 1924 and 1928. His doctoral thesis (1928) was later published as the monograph *Tribes of the Rif* (1931), and on the basis of his fieldwork Coon wrote two fictional works as well, *Flesh of the Wild Ox* (1932) and *The Riffian* (1933).[34] Coon's research in the Rif encompassed both physical and social anthropology, and a large portion of *Tribes of the Rif* is devoted to an analysis of the physical data he amassed on more than a thousand men in the Rif and elsewhere in Morocco. The monograph and Coon's novels also contain much information about social and economic structures, material culture, oral history, religious practices, and other aspects of daily life in the Rif in the early twentieth century.

After receiving his doctorate, Coon was appointed to a teaching position at Harvard, where he stayed until 1948, when he took a professorship at the University of Pennsylvania. During World War II he served in Morocco with the Office of Strategic Services, the forerunner of the CIA. A colorful description of his wartime activities can be found in his autobiography and in a full-length book he wrote about his experiences.[35] After the war Coon continued to teach and carry out archaeological and anthropological research in many parts of the world, especially Europe and the Middle East. He was a prolific writer, publishing across anthropology's subdisciplines of archaeology, physical anthropology, and social anthropology. He also wrote some popular general texts, including *Caravan: The Story of the Middle East* (1951) and *The Story of Man* (1954).[36]

In his research in the Rif, Coon's primary interest lay in trying to determine the origins of the Riffians, using the methods of physical anthropology to relate them to established "racial" categories based on physical differences. Coon had been trained as a physical anthropologist at a time when the main methodological tool was anthropometry—measurements of the head, face, and body and observations of hair, skin, and eye color. Anthropometric measurements had earlier been used to study human growth and development, but in the late nineteenth century physical anthropologists began to apply them to the study of human diversity. They saw these measurements as a valuable tool with which to define distinct racial groups more precisely, and anthropologists such as Coon set off to the far corners of the world to measure and tabulate large numbers of subjects.

Although seen as legitimate scientific practice at the time, this methodology was roundly criticized by anthropologists of later generations. Even at the time of Coon's research in the Rif, the American anthropologist Franz Boas had already argued that

physical attributes were often related to environ-
mental factors rather than being inherent racial
configurations.[37] Physical anthropologists eventually
concluded that racial groups could not be so neatly
defined, and social anthropologists argued that the
concept of race itself was flexible and socially constructed. Coon continued to study the evolution and
definition of human races throughout his career, and
although he was consistently praised for the thoroughness of his research, he also drew criticism for
some of the conclusions he reached.[38]

Carleton Coon was a student at Harvard when the
Peabody Museum and the Department of Anthropology were first establishing a group of faculty
and students to carry out fieldwork in Africa. As

Carleton Coon and an assistant at
an archaeological excavation in
Morocco in 1947. PM 2004.24.31020.

he recounted in his autobiography, his interest in the Rif was sparked by a course on
the races and cultures of Africa taught by Professor Hooton during Coon's junior year
at Harvard. According to Coon, Hooton "described in vivid terms the allegedly
blood-thirsty habits of the Riffians. They were northern Moroccan Berber mountaineers, some of whom were blond, and how they had gotten there was a mystery I
hoped to solve."[39]

It would take two exploratory trips to Morocco before Coon managed actually to
enter the Rif. On the first of these trips, in the summer of 1924, Coon and a fellow
Harvard undergraduate, Gordon Browne, traveled to Casablanca, Fes, and Taza, a
small city just south of the Rif Mountains. There they were able to explore a few caves,
but the war going on in the Rif prevented them from traveling farther into the region.
The two young men did amass a collection of Riffian-style pottery, however, which
they donated to the Peabody Museum in 1927. In the summer of 1925 Coon returned
to Morocco with Thomas Scudder, another Harvard colleague, and carried out
archaeological excavations outside Casablanca. He also began to take some anthropometric measurements. In a letter to Hooton on this topic he wrote: "Yesterday I

measured my first man, a Shawia, these are shy people but are beginning to warm up now, perhaps we can get more. The measuring game in this country is a ticklish business and I can't promise any more. Archaeology is much safer."[40]

Despite the "ticklishness" of this research methodology, Coon returned to Morocco in June 1926 with the intention of carrying out a large-scale anthropometric study and hoping finally to visit the Rif. On this trip he was accompanied by his new wife, Mary Goodale, who came along for an unconventional honeymoon. Because the Riffian leader Abd el-Krim had only recently surrendered, the region was still considered too dangerous, and the Coons began their work in Tangier. Coon was determined to get into the Rif, however, and after a few detours and false starts the couple set out on their first trip through the region on September 1, 1926. They traveled by mule, accompanied by two Riffians who had been living in Fes. In field notes written at the time and in a vivid passage in his autobiography, Coon described the people and places they visited in the mountainous area north of Taza. At each stop along the way he and Mary were the guests of local tribal leaders, who invariably greeted them with a mixture of wariness and hospitality. Explaining that they were American, not French or Spanish, generally put them in better favor with the people they met, and their cause was helped by Coon's sense of humor and Mary's compassion for the sick.

This first trip into the Rif, for which Coon had waited so long, was cut short by a blustery French army officer who insisted that the two leave immediately, before they got themselves killed. They were eventually able to return, this time with their anthropometric instruments. They traveled by much the same route north from Taza, measuring people in many of the villages they had visited before. On this second trip, in December 1926 and January 1927, they made it all the way to the coast at Ajdir, near the present-day city of Al Hoceima. They eventually continued to the city of Melilla, just north of Nador, where they stayed for almost a month measuring Riffian men at different market centers. Similar efforts in Tetouan, south of Tetouan in Chefchaouen, and during a two-month stay in and around Marrakesh gave Coon a large quantity of physical data on which to base his dissertation.

Less tangible information about the Riffians and their way of life was provided by the many people who gave the couple shelter, protection, and friendship along the way. Foremost among these was Mohammed Limnibhy, from the Igzinnayen (also spelled Gzennaya) area in the central Rif. Limnibhy had served in the French army in World War I and as a commander in the Riffian resistance under Abd el-Krim. He and the Coons met on one of the couple's first nights in the heart of the Rif, after a hard day's journey over a mountain pass had brought them to the village of Tiddest and the house of Sheikh Si Moh wild el-Hajj Bukkeish.[41] Coon had spent the evening talking and joking with the men there in broken Arabic and a few words of Tarifit, when suddenly someone addressed him in French, asking where he was from. Coon's response in less-than-perfect French apparently convinced the man that he and his wife were not French or Spanish invaders but Americans with unknown, probably harmless, intentions. According to Coon, Limnibhy saved his and Mary's lives that evening by persuading the others present that these strangers were "not foes, but friends."[42]

From that moment, Mohammed Limnibhy became the Coons' constant companion in Morocco. He traveled with them through the Rif and accompanied them during an extended stay in Marrakesh, on a trip into the Atlas Mountains, and during a brief stay in Tangier and Chefchaouen. Coon relied on Limnibhy for information about Riffian families, households, and villages; traditions related to customary law and religious practices; and oral histories that he later rewrote in his novels about the Rif. Limnibhy's role went much farther than this, however. Coon described the extent of it in his acknowledgments in *Tribes of the Rif*: "Limnibhy, as interpreter, collector of ethnological data, anthropometric assistant, blood-letter, bodyguard, and diplomat supreme, showed himself to be a brilliant field worker on his own account."[43]

Carleton and Mary Coon returned to Morocco in the spring of 1928, and Limnibhy accompanied them to the western Rif, where they visited craftsmen in Taghzuth (Coon's spelling; also spelled Tarhzout) who worked leather and made weaponry used throughout the Rif. After this brief trip, Coon arranged for Limnibhy to come to the United States with them, later writing: "I needed what lay still untapped in his head. Without him I could not have written my first three books, and I believed he might be a little safer in Massachusetts than in Morocco because of his record in the French colonial books."[44] Limnibhy lived with the Coons in Cambridge in 1928–1929,

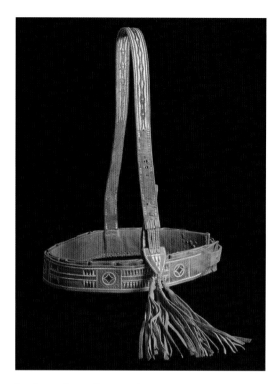

Leather and iron alloy cartridge belt (*dhaghugat er knenth*) made in Taghzuth (Tarhzout), Morocco. Leather bags, belts, and cartridge belts were important parts of Riffian men's daily attire. The leatherworkers in Taghzuth in the western Rif were especially renowned. They made items for sale throughout the region and for export to Europe and the U.S. Collected by Carleton Coon in 1926–1928. PM 30-73-50/L181 (H 98 × W 65 × D 1.5 cm). 98520059. Mark Craig, photographer.

continuing to provide the information on Riffian social structure, oral history, and material culture that Coon would use in his publications.

After Limnibhy returned to Morocco, he corresponded often with the Coons, and his letters and those of Coon's other Riffian companions are preserved in the Carleton S. Coon papers at the Smithsonian Institution's National Anthropological Archives. In October 1931 Limnibhy died under mysterious circumstances, possibly the victim of poisoning. A French army officer later told Coon that the French had ordered his death because "he had been drinking heavily, playing around with other men's wives, and generally creating unrest."[45] Whatever the reasons behind Limnibhy's death, his contribution to Coon's early work is evident, as is the strong attachment Coon felt to him and to the many other Riffians who generously gave him shelter and guidance throughout his research.

Carleton Coon donated archaeological specimens as well as contemporary pottery, woodwork, leatherwork, and clothing from the Rif and other parts of Morocco to the Peabody Museum. He acquired the majority of these objects during his doctoral field research between 1926 and 1928. Because Coon's primary interest was in the racial origins of the Riffian tribes, he used many of the objects he collected as examples of the "true" Riffian material culture that corresponded to the physical type he assumed was authentically Riffian. This was especially true of the hand-formed and hand-painted pottery made by women in the central Rif. Coon's interest in the state of Riffian technology also influenced the types of objects he collected or even commissioned. The Peabody houses, for example, a series of carved wooden spoons and a woven grass sandal, both made by Mohammed Limnibhy during his stay in Massachusetts in order to demonstrate Riffian techniques of manufacture. Coon's collection is not necessarily representative of all aspects of Riffian artisanship, but it does provide some insights into many arts that were part of daily life at the time of his research.

A large proportion of the collection from the Rif at the Peabody Museum is made up of painted pottery vessels donated by Coon and by his colleague Gordon Browne. Women in the Rif crafted pottery vessels to serve many domestic purposes, and vessels bearing the intricate designs of the central Rif are still made in some areas today (pl. 12).[46] In Coon's time this pottery was seldom sold in markets; the potters of each village normally made only enough vessels to fill local needs. Coon acquired the best examples of this type of pottery from women he met during his travels. Limnibhy's stepmother and the mother of a young man named Ali, from Ajdir, both gave him vessels that he donated to the Peabody.

Alongside women's hand-formed, painted pottery existed a parallel Riffian industry of pottery made by men on a potter's wheel, expressly for sale in local markets. These vessels were generally larger, undecorated, and used to carry and store

Water vessel with spout from the Rif, Morocco. A cone shape in the base allows the jar to fill with water when it is lowered into a well. This vessel was made by the mother of one of Carleton Coon's informants in Ajdir, who was known locally as a skilled potter. Collected by Carleton Coon in 1926. PM 27-37-50/B4329 (H 17.8 × W 16.2 × D 13.4 cm). 98520054. Mark Craig, photographer.

water or oil. A similar industry exists today in the Rif and other parts of Morocco, and archaeological evidence indicates that the use of both wheel-made and hand-formed pottery may go back as far as the first century C.E. in many parts of the Berber-speaking world.[47] Coon collected no examples of this larger, wheel-thrown pottery, but he and Browne did purchase a number of pieces that complicate a strict division between women's hand-formed and painted pottery and men's wheel-made and undecorated pottery (pl. 13). These vessels seem to have been made with a wheel but also bear the painted geometric designs typical of Riffian women's pottery. It is unclear whether these pieces were made by men, by women, or through their combined efforts, but they show an intriguing overlap in techniques that are usually separated by gender in the literature on rural North African pottery traditions.[48]

Women from Taghzuth in the western Rif wearing woven wool garments similar to those worn in the rest of the Rif and in Kabylia. Photograph taken by Carleton Coon in 1928. PM 2004.24.20558.

A similar division of labor existed in the realm of textile production in the Rif. Women worked with vertical looms to produce woolen cloth for women's garments and blankets. This cloth was usually left a natural white but was sometimes decorated in patterns of red stripes. The brown or black wool cloth used to make men's jellabas and other garments (pl. 14) was woven by men on horizontal looms. Men also sewed these garments together and embroidered them. Coon wrote that students at local mosques often made money to support their studies by sewing and embroidering men's garments.

Once imported cotton and silk cloth became widely available, both women's and men's garments began to change. Women in the Rif started to wear brightly colored cotton cloth sewn into long loose shirts that were embroidered around the neck (pl. 15). Coon described this style as taking hold only slowly, but by the 1950s these shirts and their accompanying loose trousers had become the most common form of woman's garment. The older form of dress was similar to the Kabyle *axellal*, a large rectangular piece of woven cloth held in place at the shoulders by silver brooches. Riffian brooches, too, became increasingly rare as women's clothing styles changed.[49]

Another important industry in the Rif was leatherwork. Coon described two types of leatherwork popular for Riffian men's leather bags and belts. The older style was embroidered with silk and produced in the northern Temsaman region (pl. 6); the newer style featured designs of colored leather and was produced by leatherworkers in Taghzuth, just west of Targuist (pl. 16). This second style was the most widespread at the time of Coon's research, and the craftsmen of Taghzuth produced both leather goods and weaponry for use throughout the Rif. Coon visited them during a brief trip to Morocco in 1928, when he acquired examples of leather cartridge belts (see p. 38) (see p. 38) and bags to demonstrate the sophistication of their artistry.

Coon collected other items representative of everyday material life in the Rif: carved and decorated wooden spoons, woven grass sandals, and items of clothing. Several types of Riffian craftsmanship, however, are not represented in his collection. Specialized artisans produced metal agricultural implements, tools, weapons, and silver jewelry for use throughout the Rif. Women made baskets, mats, blankets, and woven cloth for their families. Carleton Coon's collection from the Rif was shaped by his particular research interests, but it gives us a glimpse of daily life among the Riffians in the early twentieth century. As in much of the Berber–speaking world, the domestic accoutrements of the Riffian household were sparse, but the intricate decoration of these everyday objects makes them part of a larger universe of Berber symbology.

Kel Ahaggar Tuareg men, southern Algeria, 1953. Photograph by David Douglas Duncan. Photography Collection, Harry Ransom Humanities Research Center, The University of Texas at Austin.

The sober truth about the Sahara . . . is more mysterious than
anything that has ever been written about it, even by the
most irresponsible spinner of fairy-tales; for the fact is that
very little is yet known about the peoples who live there.
—Lloyd Cabot Briggs, *Tribes of the Sahara*, 1960

COLLECTING TUAREG ART

BY FAR THE MOST EXTENSIVE COLLECTION of objects from the Berber-
speaking regions of North Africa at the Peabody Museum came as a donation from
Harvard research anthropologist Lloyd Cabot Briggs. During almost fifteen years of
residence in Algeria between 1947 and 1962, Briggs acquired a large and wide-
ranging collection of material culture. Although he collected clothing, jewelry, and
other objects from Kabylia and other parts of Algeria, he ultimately focused his collecting on the Algerian Sahara, home of the Berber-speaking Kel Ahaggar Tuareg.
Briggs published widely on the prehistory and contemporary life of the Sahara, providing both scholarly and general audiences with information about the desert and its
peoples previously unavailable to an English readership. As part of this lifelong project he gathered material evidence of the Tuareg way of life, amassing a significant collection of Tuareg art that he donated to the Peabody Museum over many years. Owing
largely to his efforts, the Peabody is home to a collection of Tuareg craftsmanship
rivaling that of major ethnographic museums in Europe and Algeria.[50]

The Tuareg are Berber speakers who have lived for many centuries as pastoral nomads in the central Sahara, occupying parts of what is now Mali, Niger, Algeria, Libya, and Burkina Faso.[51] They are divided into several confederations, and scholars generally distinguish the northern Tuareg—the Kel Ahaggar and Kel Ajjer—who live mostly in Algeria, from southern groups such as the Kel Aïr in Niger and the Kel Adrar in Mali. Lloyd Cabot Briggs carried out research in the Algerian Sahara among the Kel Ahaggar, and most of the objects in his collection came from that region, although many likely were made by Tuareg artisans in northern Niger. Northern and southern Tuareg speak closely related varieties of Berber, called Tamahak in the north and Tamashek in the south. The exact derivation of the word *Tuareg* is unknown, but its origin lies in a term used by Arabs and not by Tuareg themselves. Instead they call themselves by regional names such as Kel Ahaggar (people of the Ahaggar region), by linguistic names such as Kel Tamahak (people who speak Tamahak), and sometimes by the more general name Kel Tagelmust (men who wear the veil).

This last designation calls attention to a distinguishing trait of Tuareg material culture that has fascinated outsiders for centuries. In contrast to other Muslim peoples, among the Tuareg men customarily wear a turban and face veil (called a *tagelmust*) that covers the mouth and nose, whereas Tuareg women wear a long headcloth but do not cover their faces.[52] The functions and meanings of the *tagelmust* are primarily social; it helps men maintain social distance and express respect for one another. Covering the mouth is also likely related to beliefs in the evil eye, the evil mouth, and the Kel Asouf, spirits that can enter the body through the mouth. Kel Ahaggar men today wear the *tagelmust* less frequently than their predecessors did, and it has become more a symbol of ethnic identity than an essential element in regulating social relations.[53]

Another feature that distinguishes Tuareg groups from northern Berbers is their use of a matrilineal descent and inheritance pattern. Although the Tuareg also use patrilineal forms of residence and inheritance, the importance of the mother's line of descent gives women a high-status public role that is rare in the strictly patrilineal northern Berber societies.[54] Perhaps the most salient feature of Tuareg society, however, is the importance of social stratification. Although much has changed as the traditionally nomadic Tuareg have become increasingly settled, among the Kel Ahaggar

Kel Ahaggar Tuareg women at their tent, southern Algeria, 1953. Photograph by David Douglas Duncan. Photography Collection, Harry Ransom Humanities Research Center, The University of Texas at Austin.

the two main social classes are still the Ihaggaren (nobles) and the *imrad*, or Kel Ulli (vassals). Traditionally the Ihaggaren bred camels and controlled caravan routes stretching across the Sahara, living off tribute paid by traders and vassals and profits gained by raiding weaker rivals. The Kel Ulli, literally "people of the goats," cared for livestock and produced the subsistence base for Tuareg existence. Without the goats and other resources they provided, the nobles would have been unable to survive. In exchange for products paid in tribute by the Kel Ulli, the Ihaggaren protected them from raiders.

The Kel Ahaggar also obtained agricultural products from farmers (*izeggaren* or *harratin*) who began settling in the region in the mid–nineteenth century, and the nobles were supported by a domestic working class made up of enslaved peoples (*iklan*) obtained through raiding campaigns. Another class, the *ineslemen*, served as religious teachers and advisors. In addition, the Kel Ahaggar acquired many finely crafted objects from an artisan class, the *ineden*, who produced metal, wood, and leather goods.[55]

The *ineden* (singular *ined*) lived either in agricultural centers or with Kel Ahaggar encampments, but they were considered outsiders to the Tuareg lineages. Both general handymen and accomplished artisans, they also sometimes served as healers, poets, musicians, and emissaries for their noble patrons. They were compensated for their work with a portion of the agricultural harvest, with livestock, or, later, with currency. The *ineden* married only within their class, and female *ineden* (*tineden*) specialized in fancy leatherwork and served as midwives. The *ineden* were an integral part of Tuareg society and were admired for their skills, but they were also looked down upon for engaging in manual labor and feared for the supernatural powers thought to be associated with metallurgy.

Today many *ineden* have established workshops and boutiques in cities, where they produce jewelry and other objects for both Tuareg and foreign clienteles. They may also play the role of antiques dealers, providing museums and collectors with older pieces purchased from local families. The objects produced by the *ineden*—from carved wooden ladles to elaborate camel saddles—display the Tuareg taste for beauty and embellishment in both ceremonial and everyday objects.

Even before the colonial era, Tuareg society as just described was undergoing significant changes. Older taboos on the vassal classes' owning weapons and camels began to break down in the nineteenth century, leading to important transformations in the noble–vassal relationship. French control of the region, starting with the defeat of the Kel Ahaggar at the battle of Tit, near Tamanrasset, in 1902, further reduced the Ihaggaren's traditional sources of economic and political power, for they were no longer able to control and exact tribute from the trans–Saharan caravan routes. The vassal classes no longer needed the nobles' protection, and they began to expand their economic activities through trans–Saharan salt caravans. Eventually much of the trans–Saharan trade was taken over by Europeans using trains and trucks.

United by a common language and culture but spread across national boundaries, the Tuareg have fared differently in the independent African states. In the southern

Tuareg regions, where significant political and economic changes also took place under the French, the pastoralist way of life was further devastated by the Sahelian droughts of the 1970s and 1980s. In Niger and Mali, increased marginalization and state efforts at forced settlement led to armed conflict between authorities and Tuareg resistance fighters in the 1990s. In these countries thousands of Tuareg people were displaced, moving to refugee camps or to Algeria, Mauritania, or Burkina Faso. Post-independence Algeria also discouraged nomadism and saw the stratification of Tuareg society as incompatible with the state's socialist values. Changing economic and political conditions have led many Kel Ahaggar to settle in Tamanrasset and smaller towns, while those who continue to lead nomadic lives have sought new sources of income such as tourism. According to one estimate, whereas 90 percent of the Kel Ahaggar were living nomadically at Algerian independence in 1962, probably only 10 to 15 percent do so today.[56]

These transformations in the traditional Tuareg way of life were already under way when Lloyd Cabot Briggs first visited the Ahaggar region in the 1950s. Briggs graduated from Harvard College with a degree in anthropology in 1931 and earned a certificate in anthropology from Oxford University in 1932. For a time he worked for brokerage firms in New York, but eventually he returned to the study of anthropology, receiving an M.A. from Harvard in 1938 and a Ph.D. in 1952. During World War II Briggs, like Carleton Coon, served with the Office of Strategic Services in North Africa. He was stationed in Algiers for most of the war and was awarded the Medal of Freedom for his service there. After the war Briggs resumed his studies, pursuing a Ph.D. in physical anthropology under Earnest Hooton. His doctoral dissertation focused on the prehistory of northwestern Africa, and he carried out archaeological research in conjunction with the American School of Prehistoric Research as well as osteological research using the collections of the Bardo Museum's Laboratory of Physical Anthropology and Prehistoric Archaeology in Algiers.

After completing his doctorate, Briggs remained in Algeria as a research fellow for the Peabody Museum. Over the course of his career he engaged in many research projects that showed his wide-ranging interests and scholarly thoroughness. Like Coon, who was one of Briggs's professors and mentors at Harvard, Briggs was interested in the physical anthropology of the groups he studied, but again like Coon, he wrote about social structures and daily life as well. For his monograph *The Living Races of the Sahara Desert* (1958) and a second work geared toward a larger audience, *Tribes of the Sahara* (1960), Briggs wrote that he had "threshed and winnowed all the Saharan literature that I could get my hands on."[57] He supplemented this textual research with fieldwork, especially among the Kel Ahaggar and the Chaamba, a group of Arabic-speaking pastoral nomads. His two books presented, for the first time in English, a broad overview of the physical, social, and material life of the peoples inhabiting the Sahara.

Although he was based in Algiers during his residency in Algeria, Briggs spent much of his time in the field. He visited Tamanrasset and the Ahaggar region on many occasions and also carried out an in-depth study of the Jewish community in the Saharan oasis of Ghardaïa, published as *No More For Ever: A Saharan Jewish Town* (1964).[58] When his field research was curtailed by the war for independence in Algeria (1954–1962), Briggs continued to work in his personal library and at the Bardo Museum of Ethnography and Prehistory in Algiers. In the end, political events forced him to leave the country. Briggs later wrote of his last years in Algiers that "death quite literally stalked the streets for three long and terrible years."[59] Back in the United States, he continued to publish the results of his Algerian research and founded the Department of Anthropology at Franklin Pierce College. The large collection of books, Tuareg art, and other North African objects he had brought back with him was displayed around his family home in New Hampshire until it came to the Peabody Museum in 1975 through his estate.

Lloyd Cabot Briggs was both an anthropologist and a collector, someone drawn to beautiful or significant objects. He had collected Greek and Roman coins, books, and manuscripts, but his collecting practices were most fully expressed through his interest in Tuareg arts. Because a large number of the objects in Briggs's collection came to the Peabody as part of his estate, it is difficult to determine exactly when and where many of them were acquired. An analysis of the earlier accessions, however, gives some indication of Briggs's collecting practices and sources. His collection includes objects he acquired while doing field research in the Ahaggar region as well as pieces he purchased from other collectors, especially French army officers and colonial

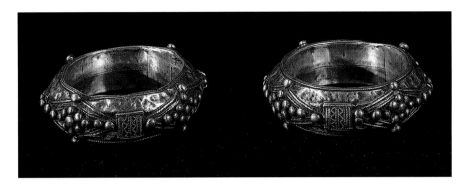

Silver alloy bracelets purchased by Lloyd Cabot Briggs in 1953 during one of his first trips to the Algerian Sahara. In museum records Briggs wrote that this type of bracelet was worn primarily by women in the oasis of In Salah. PM 53-14-50/9637 (H 7.8 × W 7.9 × D 2 cm). T4976.1. Hillel S. Burger, photographer.

administrators who had been working in the region since the early twentieth century. During the colonial period, as Kel Ahaggar nobles found it increasingly difficult to maintain their traditional way of life and their elaborate material culture, many of them turned to French administrators, foreign researchers, or the few tourists in the region to sell their finely crafted possessions. In addition, as administrative centers such as Tamanrasset grew in importance, Tuareg artisans began to make items explicitly for this clientele. Many of the important museum collections of Tuareg art, including the Peabody's, were acquired between the 1920s and the 1970s as the Tuareg adjusted to new economic and political realities.

Briggs began working in Algeria in 1948, and his earliest donations to the Peabody were items he purchased during research trips to the M'zab in the northern Sahara and other regions. In 1953 Briggs donated his first major collection of objects from the Kel Ahaggar, a group of pieces he had obtained in March that year during a trip to the Algerian Sahara. While in Tamanrasset on that trip, Briggs met up with *Life* magazine photographer David Douglas Duncan and arranged for him and some other European travelers to meet the *amenukal*, or supreme chief, of the Kel Ahaggar Tuareg. Duncan had been on a caravan through the Algerian Sahara taking pictures for a special edition of *Life* on Africa, and he gave Briggs prints of some of the striking photographs he had taken of Tuareg people.[60]

During this trip in 1953 Briggs purchased objects in the Tamanrasset market as well as from individuals. A pair of blue glass bracelets, for example, is recorded as having been purchased from the sister of the *amenukal*. On this and other research trips

Lloyd Cabot Briggs (far left) and other European travelers visiting with the supreme chief of the Kel Ahaggar Tuareg in southern Algeria, 1953. Photograph by David Douglas Duncan. Photography Collection, Harry Ransom Humanities Research Center, The University of Texas at Austin.

Briggs acquired many objects that illustrated Tuareg daily life: wooden bowls and spoons, men's veils, leather sandals, cloth dolls, and everyday jewelry such as rings and simple amulets. He also purchased more elaborately decorated items such as intricate metal locks and keys, large leather bags, and a camel saddle, as well as items used on ceremonial occasions—delicate silver jewelry, weaponry, and inscribed stone bracelets.

In addition to his own collecting among the Tuareg, Briggs acquired objects for the Peabody Museum from other collectors. French army officers, researchers, and colonial administrators had been collecting Tuareg art since the beginning of the century; many of their collections are now housed in major museums in Europe and Algeria. Briggs acquired many of his more finely crafted and prestigious objects, especially Tuareg weaponry, from other collectors. From a French army officer in Paris he purchased all the elements of a complete Tuareg tent—carved wooden poles, leather covering, and mats—which he donated to the Peabody in 1953 (pl. 17). Through his estate, the museum also received Briggs's impressive collection of Tuareg swords, daggers, spears, and shields (pls. 18, 19). Many of these objects are described and analyzed in a definitive article he wrote on Tuareg weaponry, published in 1965.[61] These weapons were likely purchased from French collectors as well.

Perhaps the most important source for Briggs's collection was Maurice Reygasse, the founder and first director of the Bardo Museum of Ethnography and Prehistory in Algiers. Reygasse had served as the French administrator in Tébessa in eastern Algeria and was an amateur archaeologist who published on the prehistory of the Sahara. In 1925 he took part in a widely publicized expedition that claimed to have discovered the tomb of Tin Hinan, the legendary ancestress of the Tuareg. Over the course of many trips to the Ahaggar region in the early twentieth century, Reygasse acquired an important collection of prehistoric artifacts as well as contemporary Tuareg art. These objects formed the basis of the Bardo Museum's collections when it was founded in 1930.

Briggs worked with these collections while researching his dissertation and became friends with Reygasse during the many years he lived in Algiers. He acknowledged his debt to his friend in *Tribes of the Sahara*: "Mr. Maurice Reygasse . . . gave me the benefit of his inexhaustible fund of miscellaneous information gathered in the course of extensive travels in the Sahara in years gone by. In many long and pleasant evenings together he drew for me pictures of the desert and its inhabitants so clear and vivid that I was reasonably familiar with many parts of the area before I ever set foot in them."[62]

Briggs purchased several objects from Reygasse's personal collection, including a finely decorated camel saddle that is recorded as having belonged to Moussa ag Amastane, the supreme chief of the Kel Ahaggar from 1904 to 1920 (pl. 20). Briggs also acquired from Reygasse pieces of leatherwork, collected between 1912 and 1930, that are examples of classic Tuareg craftsmanship and design. Along with objects clearly marked in museum records as having come from Reygasse, it is likely that other pieces in Briggs's personal collection, which came to the Peabody through his estate, were originally collected by Reygasse in the 1910s and 1920s.

Briggs's connection with Maurice Reygasse led to an interesting overlap between the Peabody's collection and that of the Bardo Museum. The two collections are similar not

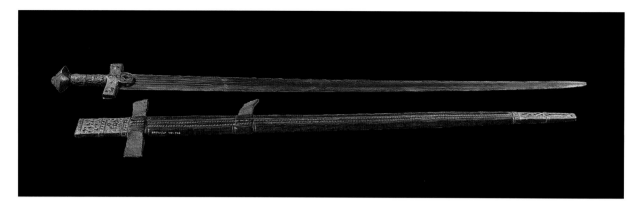

A sword (*takuba*) with a sixteenth-century, European-made steel blade (top) and its sheath, from the Algerian Sahara. The distinctive Tuareg sword is an item of great prestige. In the past swords were presented to young men as signs of their nobility and courage, and artisans devoted great attention and creativity to making them. Today swords are passed down within families and continue to be worn on ceremonial occasions. Collected by Maurice Reygasse; from the estate of Lloyd Cabot Briggs. PM 975-32-50/11868 (H 106.3 × W 10.1 × D 4.8 cm). T5048.1. Hillel S. Burger, photographer.

only in the types of objects represented but also in varieties of workmanship and design. Almost exact replicas of many of the objects donated as part of Briggs's estate can be seen in a 1959 publication cataloguing the Bardo Museum's Tuareg collections.[63] Indeed, other major collections of Tuareg material culture—at the Musée du Quai Branly (formerly the Musée de l'Homme) in Paris, the Musée d'Ethnographie in Neuchâtel, Switzerland, and the Musée Royal de l'Afrique Centrale in Tervuren, Belgium—include many of the same types of objects and designs as well.[64] These collections were all constituted in the early to mid-twentieth century during scientific expeditions in the Sahara or through the donations of military officers and colonial administrators.

A comparison of these collections reveals a kind of "canon" of Tuareg art established by early-twentieth-century collectors. The highlights of the collections, published and exhibited repeatedly over the years, are the finely crafted objects once owned by Tuareg nobles—saddles and other camel accoutrements, intricate leather bags, swords, shields, delicate silver jewelry, and locks and keys. The collections also include everyday objects such as jewelry and clothing, mats, wooden implements, and leather wallets and amulet holders, but these, too, tend to be the more elaborately decorated examples of such items.

One force shaping the establishment of this canon was the undermining of the Tuareg nobility's economic and political power during French colonial rule, which forced many economically distressed nobles to sell some of their finest possessions. This was certainly the case for many types of weaponry. In 1958 one author wrote that among the Kel Ahaggar the skin shields carried by Tuareg warriors were no longer in use, and "the last ones have been bought for museums or by collectors."[65] Another factor was that what most fascinated foreign collectors was the lives of the nobles, whom they perceived as mysterious, camel–riding warriors of the desert. Foreigners' captivation with a romantic image of the Tuareg probably impelled them to seek out weapons, camel trappings, and other elaborately decorated objects, which have come to stand for the traditional Tuareg way of life.

Although Lloyd Cabot Briggs's writings about the Tuareg call into question some of the more romantic images of them, his collection was shaped by his and other collectors' interest in the noble classes and their nomadic warrior lifestyle. Through his collection we gain a glimpse of the rich material life of the Kel Ahaggar nobility and a sense of the Tuareg taste for refined and elegant decoration. The collection also showcases the remarkable skill and craftsmanship of the Tuareg artisans who created these objects.

Most of the objects used by the Kel Ahaggar were made by members of the artisan class, the *ineden*.[66] Nevertheless, as part of nomadic society, Tuareg women of all classes manufactured certain items necessary for daily life: spoons and bowls, sacks, tent coverings, mats, cords, and storage containers for water and milk. In contrast to women in the northern Berber regions such as Kabylia and the Rif, who are still known for their skills in pottery making and weaving, Tuareg women work primarily with leather and sometimes with wood. Women of the Kel Ahaggar nobility are said to have been skilled at woodworking and to have carved designs on bowls, spoons, mortars, and tent poles (pl. 17), although today such work is done by male members of the artisan class. Tuareg women also make reed mats woven with leather strips that serve as walls to divide sections of tents and protect their inhabitants from the elements.

Men of the Tuareg noble classes were known as skilled warriors who controlled the caravan trading routes that stretched across the Sahara. Their distinctive weaponry was made by male *ineden*.[67] The most prestigious Tuareg swords and daggers were made with steel blades taken from European weapons obtained through trade and

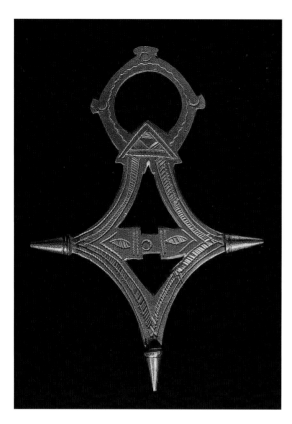

Cross pendant (*tenaghalt*) of nickel silver from the Algerian Sahara. Cross-shaped pendants were once everyday items of jewelry for Tuareg men and women. Today such pendants continue to be worn and are popular with tourists and others drawn to the distinctive work of Tuareg artisans. Collected by Lloyd Cabot Briggs in 1953. PM 53-14-50/9647.2 (H 8 × W 5.6 × D 0.5 cm). T4996.1. Hillel S. Burger, photographer.

mounted on locally fashioned hilts. The *ineden* also made their own blades, sometimes adding marks that imitated European blade-makers' marks. The leather sheaths were decorated with incised and stamped designs and with engraved metal embellishments. Swords were presented to young men as symbols of courage and nobility, and they continue to be made and worn today for special occasions.

Another distinctive piece of Tuareg craftsmanship, the saddle with a pommel in the shape of a cross (pl. 20), showcased artisans' talents in wood-, leather-, and metalworking. The most highly decorated form was made by specialized artisans in the Aïr region in northern Niger. The Kel Ahaggar also acquired decorated wooden objects (pl. 21) from these artisans, whose work was especially prized as wood became scarcer in the Ahaggar region.

The *ineden* applied their skill at metalworking to the manufacture of intricate metal locks and keys (pl. 22). These pieces, iron cases decorated with metal overlays and incised geometric designs, show the artistry used to create objects that were both practical and beautiful. Today *ineden* continue to practice their metalworking skills by making jewelry and other pieces in both silver and gold for Tuareg and non-Tuareg clients.[68] Classical Tuareg jewelry forms were primarily silver and included rings, bracelets, earrings, and pendants that were worn every day, as well as delicately decorated amulet holders (pl. 23) and larger ornaments worn only on special occasions (pl. 3). The most common form of Tuareg pendant, the "cross" shape (*tenaghalt*), was an ornament worn by both women and men. The cross pendant appears in many different forms, generally associated with different regions or Tuareg groups, and has now become both a symbol of Tuareg identity and a popular souvenir for visitors to many parts of North Africa. *Ineden* continue to make them for both local and foreign markets, and the shape is incorporated into many other objects and used in other contexts.[69]

While male *ineden* specialize in metalwork and woodwork, their female counterparts are known for their skill in making highly decorated leather items. Leather was one of the most important components of material culture for the nomadic Tuareg. Skins, generally goat but sometimes sheep or gazelle, were used to make bags, pouches, wallets, tent covers, cushions, cords, and household containers. Working collectively and with a wide range of decorative techniques, the *tineden* made a variety of objects, including large leather traveling bags decorated with colored leather appliqués, embroidery, and painted and incised geometric designs (pl. 24). Kel Ahaggar women used these bags to store clothing, jewelry, and other personal items. Today *tineden* continue to make leatherwork for a variety of markets and uses.

In addition to pieces made by local artisans, the Kel Ahaggar acquired objects made farther afield, in trading centers known for certain types of production. The distinctive green leather found on many Tuareg pieces was produced in Agadez in northern Niger, where a local supply of copper was used to make the green dye. Agadez was also the source of the molded and decorated skin boxes in which Tuareg women stored valuables such as jewelry. One type of decoration for leather bags used widely by Tuareg people was originally made primarily by Hausa women in Niger (pl. 25). Hausa artisans were also the sources of the indigo-dyed cotton that was the most prestigious type of fabric used for Tuareg men's turbans and face veils.

As a nomadic people involved in long-distance trade, the Tuareg have been directly involved in the circulation of goods, ideas, and art forms across boundaries and around the Mediterranean. Many of their beautifully crafted objects show the influence of different places and peoples, but they also bear the imprint of a specifically Amazigh aesthetic tradition. The use of geometric designs, the importance of symmetry, and the attention to embellishment despite the limits placed on material possessions by a harsh environment are all central to Berber artistic production across North Africa.

The Galerie Tamurt, one of many shops and galleries in Paris that sell contemporary Amazigh art. Photograph by Lisa Bernasek, 2006.

Amazigh Art Today

THE RICH EXAMPLES OF BERBER ARTISTIC PRODUCTION in the Peabody
Museum's collections highlight the skill and aesthetic vision of Amazigh craftsmen
and craftswomen, who work with local resources to create objects that are both beautiful and practical. These collections, acquired between the late nineteenth and the
mid-twentieth centuries, offer a glimpse of Berber life at a time when many of their
arts were under pressure to change. New products such as prefabricated cloth and
metal containers were replacing handmade goods. Foreigners were buying up older
examples of Berber art forms, and artisans were creating new pieces that appealed to
foreign tastes while preserving Amazigh artistry and symbolism. The stories I have
told so far surround the objects in the Peabody Museum, but Berber art embraces
other dimensions as well. Other regional styles exist, for example, besides those represented in the Peabody collections. I have said nothing of the art of much of
Morocco, where the majority of Berber speakers live today.

Contemporary embroidered dress, black embroidered scarf, and woven textile from Kabylia, on display at the home of Lila Ben Mamar in Paris. The textile was woven by Yamina Ben Mamar. Photograph by Lisa Bernasek, 2006.

Another important dimension is the story of Amazigh arts in the present. Far from disappearing, as many collectors feared they would, Amazigh arts continue to thrive, though sometimes in new or altered forms. Women continue to weave blankets, carpets, and other textiles, and in some regions they still produce pottery for daily use. Some Berber women still wear finely patterned woven shawls like the ones their forebears created, especially at weddings and on other festive occasions. Women also make textiles, pottery, and leatherwork to be sold in local markets and to visitors from abroad. Jewelers in Kabylia are still renowned for their fine enamel work, and Tuareg *ineden* make silver and sometimes gold jewelry both for local buyers and for foreigners drawn to their distinctive designs.

The market for Berber arts has become truly global, and products from across North Africa can be purchased in boutiques in Europe and the United States, as well as on the Internet from anywhere in the world. In addition, many types of craftsmanship have become markers of contemporary ethnic identity. Women of Kabyle origin in France and elsewhere often wear enameled silver jewelry or colorful Kabyle dresses at community events and celebrations. Patterned textiles and painted pottery may decorate homes and the buildings of Berber cultural associations in the diaspora, evoking the traditional world in a new setting.

Contemporary artists of both Amazigh and non–Amazigh ancestry also draw inspiration from older Amazigh art forms and symbols.[70] In the years following independence, artists who had been trained in European art forms created a specifically North African style by drawing on indigenous symbols such as in textile and tattoo designs. In work that has become internationally renowned, the Moroccan painter Farid Belkahia uses materials associated with artisanal production, such as skins and copper, and dyes made of saffron and henna to create canvases that often explicitly echo women's arts, especially henna painting and tattoo designs. Belkahia and the Algerian artist Rachid Koraïchi have both incorporated the Tifinagh alphabet in their work, using it as part of a geometric design vocabulary that evokes the pluriculturality of North African society. Denis Martinez, an Algerian painter of Spanish origin, also creates works inspired by Kabyle and Tuareg symbology to draw out themes of resistance and exile.

Many Moroccan and Algerian artists producing paintings and works in mixed media use their art to express a specifically Amazigh identity as well. Some artists, such as the Moroccan Mohamed Mallal, express a transnational sense of Amazigh consciousness in paintings of the Tuareg and of Saharan scenes. The use of the Tifinagh alphabet takes on a political meaning in the work of artists such as Fouad Lahbib and Mouhand Saidi. Other artists, including the Moroccan Abdallah Aourik and the Algerian Farid Belkadi, pay tribute to women's roles as guardians of Amazigh culture in paintings of women's lives, art, and work. Artists such as Hamid Kachmar, originally from southeastern Morocco but now living in the United States, draw on their sense of Amazigh identity in their choices of colors, materials, and symbols.

Although most of these artists are male, they draw on the symbolic design vocabulary of women's art and the Tifinagh alphabet to express a sense of transnational Amazigh identity. At the same time, female artisans produce traditional arts in new forms. Styles, markets, and some types of production have certainly changed, but the Imazighen and their arts continue to form an important part of the North African cultural landscape.

PLATE 1
Inscribed bracelets (*ahbeg*)
Clockwise from left: 57-36-50/
10108.1, 57-36-50/10108.3,
57-36-50/10110
Algerian Sahara
Serpentine stone
All approximately 12 × 12 × 1 cm*
Collected by Lloyd Cabot Briggs
in 1956–1957

THESE STONE BRACELETS from the Kel Ahaggar Tuareg region in southern Algeria bear inscriptions in the Berber alphabet, Tifinagh. This alphabet is related to an ancient Libyan script used as far back as the fourth century B.C.E. and known from inscriptions found on monuments at archaeological sites across North Africa, from Fezzan in the Libyan desert to the Canary Islands off the Atlantic coast of Morocco.[71] Until recently only the Tuareg used the Tifinagh alphabet; mothers taught their children how to read and write it. The literature and history of the Berber peoples, however, were not written in their own language but preserved in oral narratives and in histories written by members of other groups that have lived in North Africa since antiquity. The Tuareg used the Tifinagh alphabet only for inscriptions, dedications, and other brief texts. Today Tuareg artisans sometimes use it to sign their names on their creations. In recent years Amazigh activists in Morocco and Algeria have encouraged the adoption of this alphabet, and some Amazigh poets and other writers use Tifinagh instead of, or alongside, Roman or Arabic script. In Morocco the Tifinagh script is now being used to teach Tamazight, the standardized form of Berber, in public elementary schools.

Tuareg men wore this type of carved stone bracelet on their upper arms, and a young man traditionally received such a bracelet along with a sword during a rite of passage into adulthood. The bracelets were fashioned by male artisans, but the inscriptions were often amorous verses added by a warrior's beloved. The Tifinagh script is itself believed to have protective power, hence its use in inscriptions like these. (T4989.1. Hillel S. Burger, photographer.)

"It is I, Takounit, who has said: I claim for myself Bedda, the owner of the bracelet. Since I was born I have been fasting; now I need you to teach me to eat; now I am ill from the grief you cause me."[72]
—Inscription on a similar stone bracelet

*All measurements are given as length × width × depth at widest point.

PLATE 2
Clove necklace (*tazlagt n qrenfel*)
46-40-50/5962
Kabylia, Algeria
Imitation coral beads, cloves, paint-
ed glass beads, silver alloy, copper
alloy, enamel, coins, cotton
35 × 7.5 × 1 cm
Donated by the heirs of Charles P.
Bowditch in 1946

ACROSS NORTH AFRICA, women use many items of jewelry not only to complement their costumes and enhance their appearance but also to protect themselves from the evil eye and other malevolent forces. This necklace from Kabylia brings together a rich choice of elements considered both beautiful and protective. The pendant in the shape of a hand is one of these. The hand symbol, which appears in many forms, is considered especially effective at blocking the evil eye. The three–pronged pendants on the necklace may also evoke the fingers of the hand, or as pointed shapes they may be meant to "pierce" the evil eye. Woven into the band of the necklace are fragrant cloves, alternating with synthetic coral beads and painted glass ones. Both cloves and coral were considered to have protective effects, explaining their widespread use in Kabyle jewelry.

Cloves were also thought to be an aphrodisiac, and a necklace like this would have been worn only by a married woman. In Kabylia and elsewhere in Algeria, women also made necklaces incorporating beads fashioned from a homemade fragrant paste called *essxab*, the main ingredient of which was cloves. A woman wore

such a necklace on her wedding night, for it offered both the seductive power of the fragrant beads and the protection necessary at a time of vulnerability to the evil eye or other misfortunes. In contrast to other types of Kabyle jewelry, which were made exclusively by men, women assembled necklaces like this one according to their own tastes. (Opposite: 98520082; left: 98520081. Mark Craig, photographer.)

65

PLATE 3

Pectoral ornament
(*tereout tan idmarden*)
57-36-50/10130
Algerian Sahara
Silver alloy
21 × 20 × 2.2 cm
Collected by Lloyd Cabot Briggs
in 1956–1957

Rattle ring (*tisek*)
57-36-50/10118
Algerian Sahara
Silver alloy, tin
3.9 × 3.4 × 3.4 cm
Collected by Lloyd Cabot Briggs
in 1956–1957

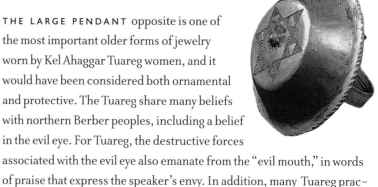

THE LARGE PENDANT opposite is one of the most important older forms of jewelry worn by Kel Ahaggar Tuareg women, and it would have been considered both ornamental and protective. The Tuareg share many beliefs with northern Berber peoples, including a belief in the evil eye. For Tuareg, the destructive forces associated with the evil eye also emanate from the "evil mouth," in words of praise that express the speaker's envy. In addition, many Tuareg practices are related to a belief in Kel Asouf, mischievous spirits who can cause illness or even death. To protect themselves, both men and women may wear metal or leather amulets that contain pieces of paper inscribed with verses from the Qur'an or another protective writing.

An elaborate ornament such as this was worn only on special occasions; it was often one of the items a man purchased for his fiancée. It incorporates a number of elements that would protect its wearer from the evil eye or spirits. Tuareg people consider the triangle especially effective against the evil eye and incorporate triangular shapes into many types of jewelry. Here the triangles are found not only in the pendants making up the piece but also in the intricate designs decorating each pendant. This type of ornament could also serve as an amulet if it held protective writings inside the silver case. In addition, the small dangling triangles make a soft clinking sound when the wearer moves, a sound said to be effective at chasing away evil spirits.

A similar effect is produced by the sound of "rattle rings," large hollow rings filled with small seeds that make a soft rattling noise when a woman moves her hands. These sounds are also considered pleasing to the ear and are an important aspect of the ability of Tuareg jewelry to enhance a woman's appearance. (Opposite: T4981.1; above: T4977.1. Hillel S. Burger, photographer.)

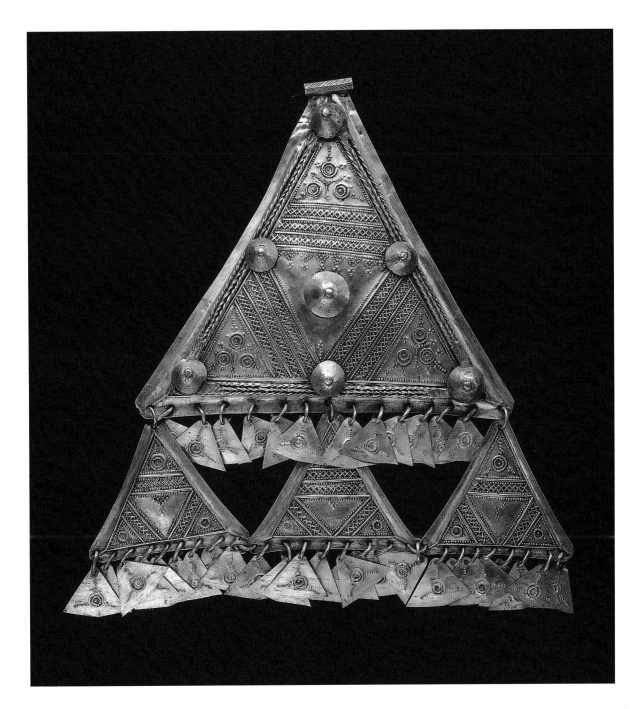

67

PLATE 4

Man's cape (*akhnif*)
45-24-50/5937
Siroua Mountains, Morocco
Goat hair, wool, cotton
188 × 170 cm
Purchased by Carleton Coon
outside Marrakesh in 1926

THIS HANDSOME CAPE, or *akhnif*, offered its wearer multiple layers of protection. Woven of heavy wool and goat hair, it literally enfolded the wearer in its warmth and shielded him from the elements. On the symbolic level, the large red shape on the back of the cloak is usually interpreted as a dramatic eye meant to protect the wearer from the malignant forces of the evil eye. The elongated pattern in the center of the red eye is sometimes called a lizard or a snake, another defensive symbol, and the other patterns woven into the cloak may have had protective as well as decorative qualities.

Cloaks like this are among the signature weavings of women of the Ait Ouaouzguite, a Tashelhit Berber-speaking group of the valleys of the Siroua Mountains, between Morocco's High and Anti-Atlas ranges. Some evidence suggests, however, that such capes were once worn by men far beyond the traditional Ait Ouaouzguite areas. Men in some regions still wear the *akhnif* today, and examples can be found for sale as collectors' items. The remarkable shape of the cloak and its red center are produced in a continuous weaving process through a complex technique of manipulating warps and adding wefts in different places. Artisans use brocading for additional decorative motifs, which vary from piece to piece.

The dramatic appearance and complex structure of the *akhnif* have caught the interest of many visitors to Morocco, and examples appear in many major museum collections. The Peabody Museum houses seven of these capes, which are sometimes known by the more general terms "burnouse" or "jellaba." Lloyd Cabot Briggs donated one, and two others came from Mrs. John Morse Elliot, who wrote to the director of the Peabody of having "caught Burnouse fever" while on a trip to Morocco in 1928. She and her husband bought two finely woven examples from Berber men on the road outside Marrakesh.[73] Carleton Coon donated four such cloaks to the museum, including this one. At least one was a practical purchase. In his autobiography, Coon recalled that before traveling by mule over the Tizi Telouet mountain pass in the winter of 1926–1927, his wife, Mary, "bought a Glawi jellaba—a good thing, for without it she might have perished from the cold before the day was over."[74] (Opposite: 98520076; left: 98520077. Mark Craig, photographer.)

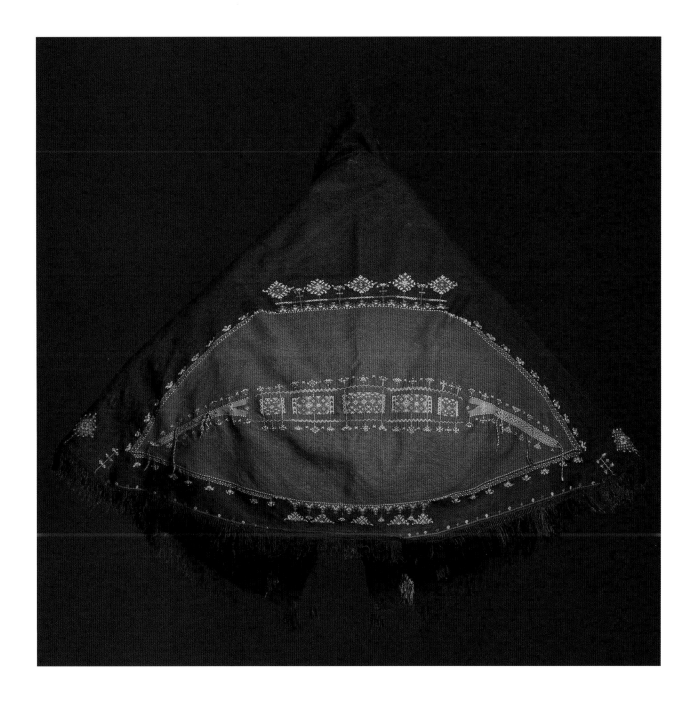

PLATE 5
Serving dish
46-40-50/5960
Kabylia, Algeria
Low-fired ceramic, mineral
pigments, natural resin glaze
10.5 × 49.1 × 46.2 cm
Donated by the heirs of
Charles P. Bowditch in 1946

SYMBOLS SUCH AS THE HAND AND THE EYE are imbued with the power to protect against the evil eye and other malignant forces, but other symbols used in Amazigh arts are less easily interpreted. This serving dish from Kabylia includes motifs from the complex design vocabulary of pottery and textile traditions. Many of the symbols have names that associate them with protective functions or with positive attributes such as fertility and abundance. The names vary from region to region, and it is impossible to know what the creator of this dish might have called them, just as her motivation for choosing them

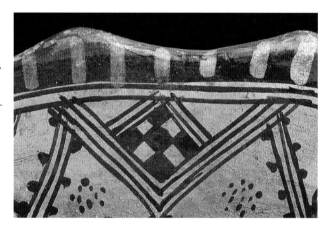

must remain a mystery. It is certain that these motifs carried symbolic as well as aesthetic power, but my interpretations, drawn from studies of Kabyle pottery symbols, are tentative.

Triangular shapes like the ones in the center of the dish are often called "fibulas," a reference to the triangular brooches Kabyle women once wore to hold their draped garments and shawls in place (see pl. 10). Both the triangular shapes and the pointed pins of these brooches are considered effective weapons against the evil eye. The diamond shapes enclosing checkerboard patterns found along the edges and in the central design are called "partridge eyes" in some regions. Birds' eyes and feet are also believed to have protective power.

Scholars of Berber art often interpret diamonds, triangles, and lozenge shapes as fertility symbols too. Polka-dot patterns like the ones decorating this dish may represent planted seeds or may be called "pomegranate seeds," and checkerboard patterns are "cultivated fields," making these patterns symbols of fertility and abundance. Motifs such as these are found frequently on vessels used for food preparation or serving. This plate would have been used to serve a communal meal of stew or couscous. (Opposite: 98520080; above: detail of 98520079. Mark Craig, photographer.)

PLATE 6

Man's leather bag
30-73-50/L184
Rif, Morocco
Leather, silk
112 × 18 × 2 cm
Collected by Carleton Coon
in 1926–1928

THIS RICHLY WORKED leather bag from the Rif incorporates many elements meant to protect its contents and its wearer from the evil eye or another misfortune. The bag's shape and complex construction guarantee that anything stored inside it will be kept safe. When it is closed, as seen at right, what looks like the front of the bag is actually a decorative panel that hides the leather pouch. The pouch, seen opposite, is folded over at the top and held shut by a strap that ties around the back. Both the front panel and the front of the pouch are heavily embroidered with symbols. Writing about Moroccan practices in the early twentieth century, Finnish scholar Edward Westermarck described many decorative motifs that could be connected to a symbolic hand or eye, both considered effective at warding off the evil eye. He argued that symbols incorporating elements of five were related to the hand, whereas diamond shapes, circles, and triangles could be read as symbolic eyes.[75] Westermarck may have overreached in his interpretations, but it is likely that many of the motifs used here had symbolic as well as decorative purposes.

Each panel on the front of the pouch bears two designs that Westermarck would have called a "double rosette" on either side of a diamond-shaped "eye" with a round pupil in its center. The four petals of each rosette, one red and one gold, are joined in the center with a circle, making up a symbol of five elements similar to that found on the Riffian pottery vessel shown on p. 13. This similarity emphasizes the common design vocabulary shared by male and female artisans, for whereas women painted pottery, men generally did the silk embroidery found on leather bags and clothing. (Opposite: 98520063, Mark Craig, photographer. Right: T4858.1. Hillel S. Burger, photographer.)

PLATE 7
Water jar
43-23-50/5841
Kabylia, Algeria
Low-fired ceramic, mineral
pigments, natural resin glaze
68.4 × 29.2 × 19.6 cm
Purchased by Mrs. Algernon
Coolidge in Kabylia in 1882

Water pitcher with spout
31-27-50/B5085
Kabylia, Algeria
Collected by Algernon
Coolidge around 1891
24.1 × 23.5 × 15.5 cm
Low-fired ceramic,
mineral pigments

IN KABYLIA, as in many other parts of North Africa, making pottery was a task women performed alongside their other domestic work. Fired pottery vessels were used for cooking, serving meals, and carrying and storing water and oil. In some villages women in each household made pieces to fill their own family's needs, but in most places a few women were known as skilled potters and produced vessels for others in return for grain or other items of barter. Beyond this local exchange, most women's pottery was not marketed, although some potters made extra pieces to be sold in local markets or through itinerant salesmen.

Although Kabyle pottery is less central to women's domestic work today than in the past, some women continue to make hand-formed and painted vessels by traditional methods, using locally gathered clay mixed with powdered pieces of used pots as temper. Pottery made by women is invariably hand shaped, sometimes with the use of a mat as a support and a piece of wood or a pebble to smooth the sides and polish the surface. Once formed, the vessel is left to dry in the sun for a few days before being painted with colors derived from locally available minerals. The traditional main colors are red and black, and the paint is applied with a bit of cloth, an animal-hair brush, or simply a fingertip. Once the painted designs are dry, the potter piles dry wood around them and fires them in the open air. Often, many women in a village fire their vessels together. The pine resin that gives some Kabyle pottery its distinctive yellow color is applied after firing, while the pot is still warm.

The painted patterns used to decorate Kabyle pottery vary from place to place. The red, yellow, and black designs on the large water jar (opposite) are associated with the villages of the At Aïssi in Greater Kabylia. The partially red-slipped water pitcher with the black-on-white pattern (above) is typical of the village of Taourirt Amokrane, also in Greater Kabylia. In the late nineteenth century these villages were easily accessible from the French administrative center, Fort National (today Larbaa Naït Irathen), a base for many tourists who explored the countryside. (Opposite: 98520073; above: 98520068. Mark Craig, photographer.)

PLATE 8
Small jar
54-42-50/9673.2
Kabylia, Algeria
Low-fired ceramic, mineral
pigments, natural resin glaze
41.5 × 19.3 × 14.2 cm
Donated by Dr. and Mrs.
Charles Brues in 1954

THE FRENCH OCCUPATION and settlement of Kabylia and the growth of tourism there in the late nineteenth century significantly affected pottery production in certain areas. According to French ethnographer Arnold van Gennep, by 1911 the people of the At Aïssi tribes, situated between the towns of Fort National (Larbaa Naït Irathen) and Tizi Ouzou, were generally using metal containers for their household needs and continued to make painted pottery primarily to meet the demands of tourists and other foreigners. This was by no means the case throughout Kabylia, and in some places pottery production for domestic use continues to some extent today. Most of the pottery pieces from Kabylia in the Peabody collections bear designs typical of the At Aïssi, however, and likely were part of the developing commerce between Kabyle potters and foreign travelers.

The new demand gave rise to new forms of vessels decorated with the red background, intricate geometric designs, and yellow pine resin varnish typical of the region. Traditional domestic forms such as two-handled water jars that evoke classical Roman amphorae were made in smaller sizes, with bases added to allow them to stand upright as decorative pieces in European homes. Artisans modeled some new forms on European-style vases and other containers. This small water jar might have been used by a young girl to carry water from a communal water source, but more likely it was made to be sold to a traveler looking for a memento of a trip to Algeria. Today pottery in a variety of forms, painted with similar designs, is sold for home decoration in Algeria and beyond.

Dr. and Mrs. Charles Brues donated this jar and three similar painted Kabyle vessels to the Peabody Museum in 1954. According to the donors, "these were the belongings of a very wealthy family, by the name of Lincoln, whose possessions were auctioned off in Forest Hills about 1924. Although there was a very extensive collection of art works . . . and much English and French Antiques these were the only pieces of such character. We have always been rather curious as to why they had them."[76] Perhaps, like many other Kabyle objects at the Peabody Museum, these pieces were acquired as souvenirs of a trip to Algeria and served for many years as ornamentation in their collectors' home. (98520087. Mark Craig, photographer.)

PLATE 9
Woman's cape (*ddil*)
41-34-50/5420
Kabylia, Algeria
Wool, cotton
122.5 × 135.5 cm
Purchased in Algiers in 1904
by Mrs. R. M. Appleton

IN KABYLIA, the loom was an integral part of the home, and traditionally all young women learned the skill of weaving from their mothers and grandmothers. Like Amazigh women in many other regions, Kabyle women made both plain and decorated woolen cloth that served as clothing, blankets, and floor coverings. The vertically mounted, single-heddle loom still used by Kabyle women is similar to looms found in other Berber-speaking regions. Wool came from local flocks, and weavers dyed it using natural and, later, chemical dyes. In some areas garments were dyed only after they were woven.

The main handwoven women's garments in Kabylia were the *axellal* and the *ddil*. The *axellal* was a long, rectangular piece of wool cloth. It was generally left a natural white, though it could also be decorated in geometric patterns or in stripes of colored wool and white cotton. It was draped horizontally around the body and held in place by large triangular brooches (pl. 10) and a woolen belt. The piece pictured here is a *ddil*, a smaller, almost square garment that covered the back all the way to the ground. It, too, was worn with brooches and a belt. The internally patterned lines ran vertically down the back, with the large section of diamond shapes in the center. In this piece, fine strands of blue, red, brown, and white wool are incorporated in a delicate tapestry weave and combined with white cotton threads to form geometric brocade patterns. The design is typical of Greater Kabylia, but the use of certain motifs—diamonds, triangles, and V shapes—recalls Berber patterns from other regions and other art forms.

By the late nineteenth century, Kabyle women were using imported cotton cloth in addition to wool fabrics made at home. The *taqendurt*, a brightly colored cotton garment sewn into a wide dress with long sleeves and an embroidered front panel, was worn along with the *axellal* and the *ddil* as an extra layer. Eventually, ready-made dresses largely replaced handwoven garments. Although Kabyle women no longer wear woven pieces like the one shown here, textiles with similar patterns and colors continue to be made in certain parts of Kabylia for use as blankets and decorative coverings. (Opposite: 98520069; left: 98520070. Mark Craig, photographer.)

PLATE 10

Triangular brooches (*abzim* or
afzim, pl. *ibzimen* or *ifzimen*)
46-40-50/5966
Kabylia, Algeria
Silver alloy, enamel, imitation coral
(modern synthetic polymer)
16 × 8 × 0.5 cm
Donated by the heirs of
Charles P. Bowditch in 1946

Inset: Reverse sides of the
brooches

TRIANGULAR BROOCHES like these, which held Kabyle women's woven wool garments pinned at the shoulders, are similar to brooches worn by Berber women in other parts of Algeria and Morocco. Kabyle jewelers passed their craft from father to son, and in the late nineteenth century the villages of the At Yenni, located near the French administrative center of Fort National (Larbaa Naït Irathen), were especially well known for their skilled artisans. In these villages, specialists produced jewelry to meet the demands of purchasers from across Greater Kabylia. The area is still known as a center for jewelry production.

Kabyle jewelry, like jewelry throughout the Berber-speaking world and in rural North Africa generally, is almost exclusively of silver. Artisans create new pieces by melting down silver coins, older pieces of jewelry, or scrap silver. Kabyle craftsmen are known for their expertise in enamel work and decorate many of their pieces on both sides with green, blue, and yellow enameled patterns. Kabyle jewelry is also recognizable by its frequent use of coral, which people once harvested in large amounts along the eastern coast of Algeria. By the end of the nineteenth century craftsmen were using synthetic materials as well, the choice between natural coral and synthetic red stones depending largely on the purchaser's budget. Patterns of enamel work, coral, and other elements on jewelry often varied from village to village, and jewelers typically followed the style requested by the client commissioning the piece. (Opposite: 98520084; inset: 98520083. Mark Craig, photographer.)

In the village of the Beni Yenni I made some purchases—a man who was working on a sewing machine (think of a sewing machine on the very top of one of the most precipitous of the peaks of the Atlas Mts.) stopping his work to allow the machine to be made use of as a show counter. . . . [One of the jewelers] had been in London and spoke a little English. He had not been in Chicago as a fellow townsman of his had, who I found in a little room here,— a room which had his bed, showcase, his fire, forge and tools in a space of 12 x 12, and not a window in it either I think. I have promised to visit him again tomorrow and to make a few last purchases of him.
—Charles P. Bowditch, 1902[77]

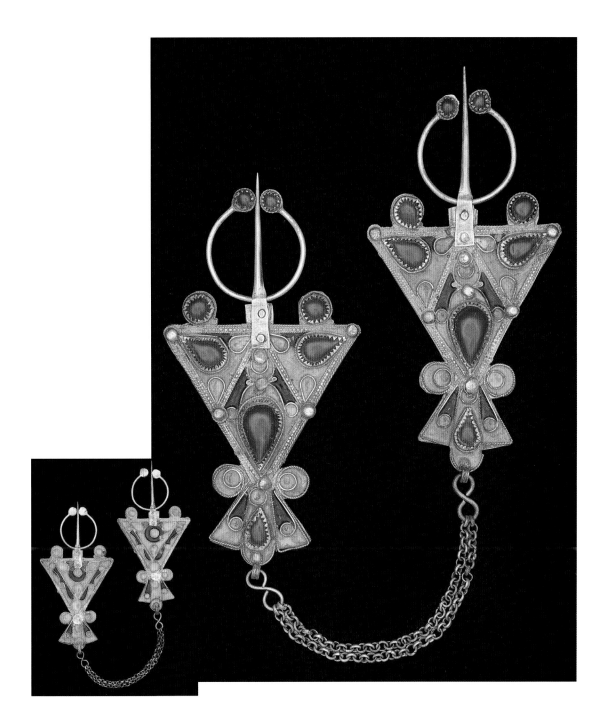

PLATE 11
Head ornament (*taᶜeṣṣabt*)
46-40-50/5970
Kabylia, Algeria
Silver alloy, enamel, imitation coral
(modern synthetic polymer)
46.7 × 16.4 × 0.7 cm
Donated by the heirs of Charles P.
Bowditch in 1946

IN KABYLIA, as in other parts of North Africa, jewelry served as a form of women's wealth. At the time of a woman's marriage, her family purchased a set of jewelry using some of the money customarily given by her fiancé's family. This jewelry remained her personal property, and she could use it as capital if she were widowed or divorced. In Kabylia the pieces most often purchased for a woman's wedding were a pair of large triangular brooches and a head ornament like this one, which the bride wore wrapped around her forehead and pinned to a headscarf. She might also receive earrings, bracelets, anklets, and necklaces. In some areas the family also bought a circular brooch at the time of a woman's marriage (see illustration on p. 27). In others the husband traditionally gave his wife this piece upon the birth of their first son. After her wedding a Kabyle woman wore only one or two pieces of jewelry as part of her everyday garb, reserving her most precious ornaments for religious festivals and other special occasions.

As fashions and economic conditions changed in the nineteenth and early twentieth centuries, traditional Kabyle jewelry underwent transformation as well. Jewelers began creating smaller pins, earrings, and other pieces to appeal to changing local tastes, although they still produced the older, larger styles when Kabyle or foreign purchasers wanted them. Visitors to the region at the time were especially drawn to Kabyle jewelers' products, and some artisans began to introduce new forms to appeal to these clients. A 1908 guidebook mentioned, for example, "the Beni-Yenni tribe, famous for the manufacture of Kabyle jewellery, photo-frames, etc."[78] Today Kabyle jewelers continue to create a wide variety of pieces in the region's signature silver, coral, and colored enamel designs. Many of the older forms and styles are worn on special occasions such as weddings. Jewelry remains an important marker of Kabyle identity for women in Algeria and in the Kabyle diaspora in France and elsewhere. (98520086. Mark Craig, photographer.)

The women all try to wear jewelry of some kind and I have not quite ruined myself in buying samples, both of the new make and of that which has been worn and which is called "ancien."
—Charles P. Bowditch, 1902

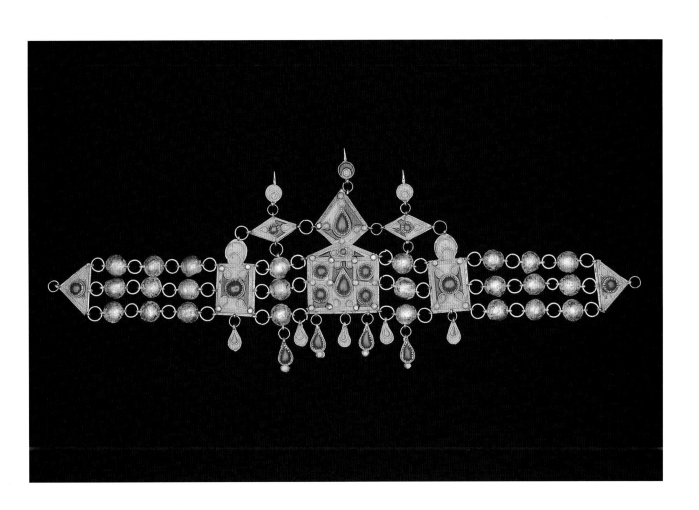

Milk pot
27-37-50/B4358
Rif, Morocco
Low-fired ceramic, natural
pigments, straw handle
20.5 × 19 × 22 cm
Collected by Carleton Coon
in 1926

LIKE WOMEN IN KABYLIA, Riffian women made hand-shaped and hand-painted pottery vessels to serve many household purposes. Riffian pottery is known for its intricate painted designs and graceful shapes. In some places women still make such pottery for domestic or decorative use; it can be found in some local markets and in shops in larger cities such as Fes. Women in the Rif use techniques much like those used in Kabylia, but the forms and decorations of their pots are distinct. They mix local clays with pieces of used pots or crushed stone as temper and form the clay into shapes typical of each local area. These include shallow plates, two-handled "milk pots" with wide mouths, and drinking vessels of various shapes. The pieces are first dried in the sun, then baked in the open air or in a mud oven, and painted. The brown patterns typical of the central Rif were traditionally made using a juice from the mastic tree, but chemical paints are now used as well. The painted pots are then fired again, which sets the design and turns the paint a deep brown or black.

Hand-shaped and painted pottery was one of the aspects of material culture that Carleton Coon identified with the central Rif region, and he collected some fine examples as part of his doctoral field research. He purchased some of these pieces in local markets and received others as gifts from people he met on his travels. Coon most likely purchased this piece at a weekly market in Temsaman, in the northern Rif. Other finely painted examples came from Mohammed Limnibhy's stepmother and from the mother of a young man named Ali who also helped Coon with his research (see illustration on p. 30).[79] (Opposite: 98520055; left, reverse of pot: 98520056. Mark Craig, photographer.)

IN THE RIF and elsewhere in the Berber-speaking world, women and men often produce two types of pottery side by side. While women make hand-formed and decorated pottery for cooking, drinking, and eating, men use a potter's wheel to throw larger vessels for carrying and storing water and oil. Unlike most women's pottery, these wheel-made vessels are produced in specialized workshops expressly for sale in local markets and beyond. Most of the rural men's pottery is undecorated, but exceptions exist.

These two painted vessels, purchased by Carleton Coon and Gordon Browne in 1924, seem to be among the exceptions. Their interiors show wheel striations, but their exteriors bear the painted geometric designs typical of women's pottery from northern Morocco. Museum records reveal that Coon and Browne purchased the pieces in the Zerhoun region, outside of Meknes—they were unable to visit the Rif during this trip—and that the pots were made by members of the Riffian Axt Tuzin tribe. According to Coon, the men of the Axt Tuzin and neighboring tribes were known to make wheel-thrown pieces that imitated the shapes and painted designs typical of women's pottery. He was likely referring to the pieces pictured here when he wrote:

> The shapely designs of the central Riffian ware . . . are copied on the wheel in certain tribes adjacent to the central Riffian area. The design typical of the Rif is put on, a little too perfectly to be true, and the product is sold in markets as Riffian pottery. This hybrid type is made, not as a survival of Riffian design in an area of recent adoption of the wheel, but as a definite attempt to imitate and defraud.[80]

Coon did not elaborate on whom the artisans were "defrauding," but it seems likely that the injured parties were not local consumers, but visitors to the region who thought they were buying "typical" Riffian pottery. Perhaps these pieces, instead of being seen as frauds, should be read as creative adaptations by local artisans looking for new markets for their goods. Whatever the origin of this style, the pieces cannot simply be dismissed as imitations, and their existence gives us new perspectives on "traditional" Riffian pottery. (Opposite: 98520052; above: 98520053. Mark Craig, photographer.)

87

PLATE 14

Jellaba

30-73-50/L189

Rif, Morocco

Wool, cotton, silk

147.5 × 157 cm

Given to Carleton Coon by
Mohammed Limnibhy in
1926–1928

MOHAMMED LIMNIBHY, a well-traveled Riffian whom Carleton Coon met on one of his first nights in the region, served as Coon's research assistant in Morocco and gave him a great deal of information on the less tangible aspects of life in the Rif. He was also a valuable resource for Coon's research on Riffian material culture. This jellaba originally belonged to Limnibhy; he gave it to Coon, who donated it to the Peabody Museum in 1930. The museum also houses objects made by Limnibhy while he lived in Cambridge in 1928–1929, including a sandal he wove out of American marsh grass to demonstrate one of the typical sandal types made and worn in the Rif. In his autobiography Coon wrote: "The *khalifa* [of Telouet, south of Marrakesh] asked Limnibhy for his Riffian jellaba, but Limnibhy said he had promised it to me. So he had, but I had mentally promised it to the Peabody Museum, where it was still hanging the last time I went up to the exhibits on the fourth floor."[81]

The jellaba, a long robe with sleeves and a hood, is a garment found throughout North Africa. Today both men and women wear jellabas in various materials and styles, but in the Rif at the time of Coon's research they were worn only by men. The Riffian jellaba is distinguished by its embroidery patterns and shorter length, falling only to mid–calf. The brown wool cloth used to make jellabas in the Rif in the early twentieth century was woven by men on a horizontal loom, whereas the white or striped cloth for women's garments and blankets was made by women on a vertical loom. The silk embroidery decorating the hood, the front seam, and the sleeves was also men's handiwork. (Opposite: 98520064; above: 98520065. Mark Craig, photographer.)

The men wore jellabas, brown, gray, black, or striped, with Berber patterns woven in, and embroidered in many col-
ors along all the seams, also with the usual colored tufts of thread. Perhaps in the designs one could find some traces
of Tafinaq [the Tifinagh alphabet]. Everybody seemed well dressed, but these clothes always look well no matter what
their age and condition.
—Carleton S. Coon, 1927[82]

89

PLATE 15

Woman's shirt (*dhaidhwarth*)
45-24-50/5936
Rif, Morocco
Cotton, silk
129.5 × 150.5 × 0.3 cm
Made by students at the mosque in
a village in the Igzinnayen region
Collected by Carleton Coon in
1926–1928

CARLETON COON donated items of clothing from both rural and urban Morocco to the Peabody Museum. This woman's embroidered shirt is one of the few items from the Rif, and Coon probably collected it during one of his trips there in 1926–1927. At the time of his visit, Riffian women's costume was undergoing changes similar to those described for women's dress in Kabylia. The older form of women's clothing in the Rif was similar to the Kabyle *axellal*—a large rectangular piece of hand-woven wool cloth worn wrapped around the body and held in place by brooches and a woven belt (see illustration on p. 40). In addition, women in the Rif often wore a square woolen shawl, frequently decorated with red stripes, wrapped around the shoulders or covering the head.

The woman's shirt pictured here was a clothing style that was coming into fashion at the time of Coon's research in the region, although it had not completely replaced the older woolen garments. It is made of imported cotton cloth sewn into a long, loose shirt with long sleeves. It would have been worn with wide cotton trousers and a red wool belt made in Spain. The embroidery on the shirt was done by students at the mosque in one of the villages Coon visited in the central Rif. According to Coon, the students often produced men's garments and embroidery in order to support their studies. (Opposite: 98520074; right: 98520075. Mark Craig, photographer.)

> The garments of men are tailor-made by ṭolba, *or students in the mosque, and women's garments must be made by the women themselves, although often men who have been students and have learned the art of embroidery make and embroider their wives' garments for them.*
> —Carleton S. Coon, *Tribes of the Rif,* 1931

PLATE 16
Man's leather bag (*dhazaᶜbutsh*)
30-73-50/L183
Rif, Morocco
Leather, silk, wax, glass beads,
cowrie shell, coins, hedgehog jaw
56 × 31.5 × 3.1 cm
Made in Taghzuth
Collected by Carleton Coon
in 1926–1928

LEATHER BAGS SUCH AS THIS were integral parts of Riffian men's attire when Carleton Coon worked in the Rif in the 1920s. He described the leatherworkers of Taghzuth (Tarhzout), just west of Targuist, as the main producers of the leather belts, bags, and cartridge belts men wore throughout the region. These craftsmen specialized in the colored leather inlays seen on this bag and in the cartridge belt shown on page 38. Leatherworking was an exclusively male occupation in the Rif and throughout Morocco and continues to be an important craft in many regions today. Urban centers feature their own types of leather production, including the delicate "morocco" used for bookbinding. In the Rif at the time of Coon's research, leatherworkers concentrated on producing articles of everyday use, although they also made watchbands to be sold to Spanish soldiers and hand-bags to be exported to Europe and the United States.

Coon most likely acquired this bag during a trip to Morocco in the spring of 1928 when he, his wife, Mary, and Mohammed Limnibhy traveled to the western Rif to see craftsmen at work. The rich array of protective charms tied into its fringes attests that it had been much used before Coon acquired it. The charms include a hedgehog jaw, a cowrie shell, coins, and blue and yellow glass beads, all items that could attract the first and most harmful glance of the evil eye away from the object or person being protected.[83] (Opposite: 98520062; above: 98520060. Mark Craig, photographer.)

> *The old style bags used in the days of the flintlock rifle were very large and contained many pockets, in which were kept powder, lead balls, emergency rations, knives, papers, and other small objects which among us would be carried in pockets.*
> —Carleton S. Coon, *Tribes of the Rif,* 1931

PLATE 17

Tent poles
Opposite: 997-29-50/12576
Niger
Wood, metal repair
102.4 × 16.5 × 3 cm
Donated by Mark Rapoport
in 1997

Right: 53-51-50/9773.1
Algerian Sahara
Wood, carved and burned
decoration
169.5 × 9 × 8.2 cm
Purchased by Lloyd Cabot
Briggs from a French army
officer in 1953

FOR THE NOMADIC TUAREG, the tent was an essential part of material life. They created new tents on the occasion of a wedding, and setting up the tent was an integral part of the wedding ceremony. The women of Kel Ahaggar Tuareg encampments sewed together goatskin tent covers as a communal activity. The covers were supported by a central pole with a ridgepiece, and exterior poles were attached to the cover with cords. Shorter poles supported the mat walls that protected the tent's occupants from the elements (see illustration on p. 45). Members of the artisan class, or *ineden*, carved the wooden tent poles and decorated them with incised and burned designs. Women of the Kel Ahaggar nobility are also said to have been skilled at this type of woodworking. Women sometimes carved Tifinagh inscriptions, generally protective words or phrases, into the poles or the ridgepiece.[84]

The long pole at right, from the Kel Ahaggar Tuareg area, is part of a complete Tuareg tent—poles, leather cover, and woven mats—that Lloyd Cabot Briggs purchased from the collection of a French army officer in Paris. When Briggs donated the tent to the Peabody Museum in 1953, director J. O. Brew called attention to it in his annual report, calling it "the finest example of this type of habitation ever brought out of the desert."[85]

The shorter tent pole opposite, from the Kel Denneg Tuareg in Niger, shows a different regional style. The Kel Denneg used leather tents similar to the Ahaggar type just described, and this pole would have been used to support the mat wall of the tent. The metal repair is a testament to the value such a beautifully carved wooden object held in a region where wood was scarce. (Opposite: T4995.1; right: T5003.1. Hillel S. Burger, photographer.)

PLATE 18
Arm dagger (*telek*) and sheath
975-32-50/11872
Algerian Sahara
Steel, wood, leather, brass, iron
European blade, probably northern
Italian, around 1600
51.3 × 8.6 × 8.8 cm
Collected by Maurice Reygasse;
estate of Lloyd Cabot Briggs

TUAREG MEN OF THE NOBLE CLASSES were known as skilled warriors and owned elaborate sets of weaponry used in combat and as signs of prestige. These objects included large leather shields (pl. 19), iron lances, long swords (see illustration on p. 52), and arm daggers, all made by members of the artisan class. With French control of the Sahara, much of Tuareg weaponry was relegated to ceremonial use. The sword, which has retained many of its symbolic meanings, is the primary weapon still made and worn today. Receipt of a sword marks a young man's entrance into adulthood, and swords remain important family heirlooms and symbols of Tuareg identity.

Like many other American and European collectors, Lloyd Cabot Briggs was intensely interested in Tuareg weaponry. After studying his own collection and those of museums in France and Algeria, he wrote an authoritative article on the provenance of the blades used in Tuareg swords and daggers. On the older and most valued Tuareg weapons, the blades were of European origin, and their engraved markings allowed Briggs and other scholars to trace them to specific regions and times, if not to specific European blade makers. The Tuareg traded directly with Portuguese merchants in Mauritania as early as the fifteenth century and most likely acquired sword blades through this trade or through the trans–Saharan trade originating on the Mediterranean coast. Members of the Tuareg artisan class mounted the European blades on hilts and fashioned highly decorated sheaths to cover them.

This arm dagger would have been worn on the inside of the left arm with the handle facing downward, allowing it to be drawn easily from its sheath in the midst of battle. From its markings Briggs identified its blade as northern Italian, probably made around 1600. The blade is mounted between two plates of iron decorated in a geometric pattern—the work of a Tuareg artisan. The wooden handle is wrapped in brass wire, and the leather sheath bears a decorative pattern of punched holes that allow the green leather underneath to show through. This style of dagger was most common among the Kel Ajjer, a Tuareg group living east of the Kel Ahaggar in Algeria. (T4834.2. Hillel S. Burger, photographer.)

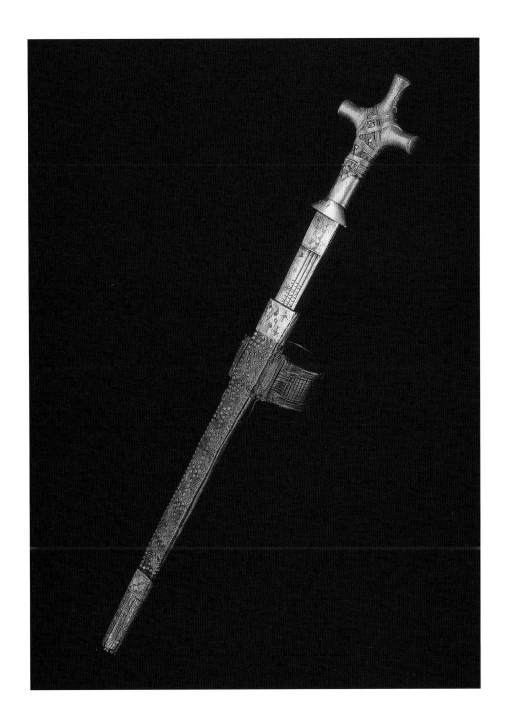

PLATE 19

Shield (*agher*)

975-32-50/11886

Algerian Sahara

Oryx skin, leather, wool, cotton, iron alloy

119.4 × 71.1 × 4 cm

Estate of Lloyd Cabot Briggs

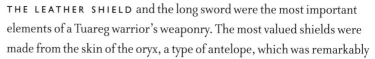

THE LEATHER SHIELD and the long sword were the most important elements of a Tuareg warrior's weaponry. The most valued shields were made from the skin of the oryx, a type of antelope, which was remarkably hard and impenetrable once tanned and dried. Large enough to cover a man's entire body, these shields could deflect sword blows and even thrown lances. When not in use they hung suspended from the warrior's camel saddle; in battle fighters held them in the left hand. Their resistant properties proved less effective in combat with French soldiers and their firearms, and by the 1950s the Tuareg no longer used shields except in ceremonies and as markers of status. The increasing scarcity of oryx also led to a steep decline in their production.

Decorative elements on Tuareg shields vary from piece to piece, but the central incised motif seen on this shield appears in some form on most of them. This motif is generally interpreted as having protective properties, although its exact origin and meaning are unclear. Some researchers see in it a series of Tifinagh letters juxtaposed to form a protective phrase; others interpret it as a local version of the "bird's foot," a protective symbol common in other parts of the Berber-speaking world.[86] The basic form of the motif bears a clear resemblance to the Tifinagh letter ⵣ (z), now used as a symbol of Amazigh identity. As in many other Tuareg arts, the written language has surely left its imprint on the decorative one.

In addition to the incised geometric designs, this shield is richly ornamented with colored leather, red cloth, and metal rivets. Shields decorated with red wool cloth became popular after French troops arrived in the region; the cloth is said to have come from French army uniforms. A similar shield is found in the collections of the Bardo Museum in Algiers. Perhaps Lloyd Cabot Briggs acquired this one from Maurice Reygasse, the French administrator and collector who was the source of most of the Bardo's collection and much of Briggs's as well. (Opposite: 98520088; above: 98520089. Mark Craig, photographer.)

PLATE 20
Camel saddle (*tarik* or *tamzak*)
975-32-50/11927
Algerian Sahara
Leather, rawhide, wood, parchment
or vellum, wool, silk, tin-plated
metal, brass-plated metal, iron,
copper alloy, cheetah skin
75 × 71 × 46 cm
Collected by Maurice Reygasse
in 1921–1922; estate of
Lloyd Cabot Briggs

THE DISTINCTIVE CAMEL SADDLE with a pommel in the shape of a cross has become an iconic symbol of Tuareg society. Saddles were essential to the Tuareg's nomadic life and are still sold in local markets. The most elaborate and sought-after ones testify to the skill of the specialized artisans around Agadez and In Gall who make them. Not all saddles are as richly decorated as this one—its elaborate metal and leather embellishments, as well as its cheetah-skin cover, signal the high status of its owner.

To create such a saddle, the craftsman fastens the pieces of the wooden base together with rawhide and covers them with tanned and painted leather. He adds metal, colored leather, cloth, and embroidery embellishments

according to his taste or that of the person commissioning the piece. This type of saddle is only used by men and is placed in front of the camel's hump; the rider's bare feet rest on the curve of the camel's neck. Women's saddles are larger, with plenty of room for stuffed leather cushions to soften the ride.

Lloyd Cabot Briggs purchased this saddle from Maurice Reygasse, who bought it after the death of its owner, Moussa ag Amastane. Amastane was the *amenukal*, or supreme chief, of the Kel Ahaggar at a critical juncture in their history. He courageously led them in battle against French forces at Tit in 1902, and after their devastating loss he negotiated peace with the French administration. He was made *amenukal* by both the French and the Kel Ahaggar in 1904. In 1916–1918 he joined with the French to defeat the Kel Ajjer, a Tuareg group living east of the Ahaggar. At the time of his death in 1920 he ruled over a large territory encompassing Ahaggar, Djanet, and much of northern Niger. (Opposite: T4837.2; left: T4994. Hillel S. Burger, photographer.)

What does a nobleman want? A white camel. A red saddle. His sword. And the song of the court of love [ahal].[87]
—Tuareg saying

PLATE 21
Wooden ladle (*tamulat*)
975-32-50/11889B
Algerian Sahara
27.9 × 9.2 × 6.4 cm
Estate of Lloyd Cabot Briggs

Wooden bowl
999-34-50/12862
Niger
Wood, metal repairs
13.5 × 23.7 × 23.4 cm
Donated by Mark Rapoport
in 1999

THOUGH PERHAPS LESS ROMANTIC than a sword or a camel saddle, this wooden ladle and carved bowl demonstrate the Tuareg artisan's attention to beauty and to embellishing even the most mundane objects. Wood is a scarce commodity in the deserts where the Tuareg live, and people highly valued wooden objects, especially before the arrival of imported metal containers. Items requiring large pieces of wood, such as bowls and tent posts, were often repaired so that they lasted for many years. This wooden bowl from the Tuareg areas of Niger has been repaired in many places with metal staples.

Male artisans are still the main producers of wooden implements, which include carved and decorated bowls, ladles, cups, mortars and pestles, and tent posts. At one time Kel Ahaggar women made everyday wooden objects as well, but as wood became scarce in the Ahaggar region, people began to obtain such objects from artisans to the south and east. The type of ladle pictured here was highly prized among the Kel Ahaggar; it was probably created by artisans around Agadez. To create such a ladle, the craftsman first shapes the form with an adze and then refines the piece by carving it with a sharp knife. It is then blackened with smoke in certain areas, and a decoration of fine lines is applied using the tip of a knife passed through a flame. In the final step the craftsman polishes the piece with butter to give it luster and bring out the incised design.

This ladle would have been used as a drinking spoon and to serve milk or soup. The accompanying bowl is from Niger and has been used (fairly recently, considering its pungent smell) to store and serve milk products. It was donated to the Peabody Museum by Mark Rapoport in 1999. Rapoport's collection of everyday objects—tent poles (pl. 17), wooden utensils, mats, jewelry, and leatherwork—from the Tuareg of Niger added a distinctive regional style to the Peabody Museum's collection of Tuareg art. (Opposite: 98520090, Mark Craig, photographer. Above: T5047.1, Hillel S. Burger, photographer.)

PLATE 22

Lock (*tanast*) and key (*asrou*)
975-32-50/11896
Algerian Sahara
Iron alloy, copper alloy,
aluminum(?)
18.9 × 14 × 3.6 cm
Estate of Lloyd Cabot Briggs

Veil weight (*asrou n'swoul*)
975-32-50/11901A
Algerian Sahara
Iron alloy, copper alloy, leather,
aluminum(?)
20 × 6.8 × 2.9 cm
Estate of Lloyd Cabot Briggs

THE TUAREG USE intricate metal locks to close the large leather bags (pl. 24) in which they store clothing, jewelry, and other personal items. These locks are made by *ineden*, male artisans who specialize in metalwork and woodwork, and the complex mechanics and delicately incised metal overlay of a lock showcase an artisan's talent and creativity. A cast-iron case contains the lock mechanism and is decorated with overlays of tin, copper, brass, and aluminum. Each lock is designed to be opened only by its corresponding key; the more complex mechanisms require two, three, or even four keys inserted in sequence. Many locks also include elements that disguise the lock mechanism or key entrance.

In the lock pictured opposite, the row of rings along the top edge covers the entrance for the key. The open rectangles on the key connect with the lock mechanism inside the case to release one side of the lock. Once the clasp is open, the rigid bar of the lock can be inserted into holes punched in the top of the leather bag. Then the lock is closed again, securing the bag's only opening. This lock and its corresponding key are particularly beautiful examples of the use of colored metal overlay and incised geometric designs. In the decorative motifs one sees echoes of symbols found in Berber art forms from other regions.

Some of the larger and more ornate keys have been elevated to the status of ornament. The key pictured at left was probably not functional but would have been tied to one corner of a woman's large headcovering to act as a weight and hold it in place. The veil weight, called *asrou n'swoul*, or "the key that is thrown over the shoulder," is a symbol of a woman's status, much like a precious piece of jewelry. (Opposite: T5000.1; left: T4999.1. Hillel S. Burger, photographer.)

PLATE 23
Double amulet necklace (*tcherot*)
975-69-50/11944
Niger
Silver alloy, copper alloy, iron alloy,
cotton, leather
11.5 × 10 × 1.3 cm
Purchased by Mr. and Mrs. Robin H.
Mix in Agadez, Niger, around 1975

JEWELRY IS AN ESSENTIAL PART of everyday dress for Tuareg people. Both women and men wear amulets, bracelets, and rings. Women also wear earrings, necklaces, head ornaments, and veil weights (pl. 22). On special occasions a woman wears all her finest jewelry, adding a large chest or head ornament, many rings, and larger bracelets to her everyday items. Jewelry is given to girls by their parents, passed down from mother to daughter, and purchased for a woman's wedding. It also serves as a form of family wealth—during times of plenty, a family might purchase jewelry that could later be sold if times grew hard.

Making jewelry is one of the many roles performed by members of the Tuareg artisan class. Like jewelry from other parts of the Berber-speaking world, Tuareg jewelry is made primarily from silver, although today Tuareg artisans also use gold to create new designs that are especially fashionable in urban areas. To create a new silver piece, the artisan melts silver thalers or other coins, older jewelry, or other pieces of scrap silver. The silver is either forged or cast using the lost-wax process, depending on the shape to be made. The piece is then decorated with engraved, punched, or repoussé geometric designs. Although many older forms of jewelry, such as the large pectoral ornament shown in plate 3, are now made only infrequently, Tuareg artisans continue to make their intricate jewelry for both local and foreign clienteles.

This amulet necklace from Niger is not only a beautiful ornament but also served a protective purpose. Tuareg men and women often wear silver amulets containing verses from the Qur'an or other protective writings on slips of paper hidden inside the delicately punched and incised case. Silver amulets come in a large variety of forms and decorative patterns. Some are decorated even more elaborately than this one; others may be simple silver squares or leather pendants or pouches. This amulet was purchased by Robin and Kendall Mix in Agadez, Niger, around 1975. The Mixes donated some beautiful examples of Tuareg leatherwork and silver jewelry from Niger and Mali to the Peabody Museum. Many of these pieces were probably Tuareg family heirlooms that had to be sold at a time of political and economic crisis.[88] (T4982.1. Hillel S. Burger, photographer.)

PLATE 24
Woman's leather traveling bag
(*tehaihait*)
975-32-50/11911
Algerian Sahara
Goat leather, cotton
137 × 111 × 16 cm
Estate of Lloyd Cabot Briggs

LEATHER OBJECTS WERE IMPORTANT PARTS of material life for the nomadic Tuareg. Like other Tuareg groups, the Kel Ahaggar seldom used the pottery containers and woven textiles so common among the settled agriculturalists of the Rif and Kabylia. If necessary they acquired pottery vessels, woven blankets, and carpets through trade, but leather and wooden objects served many of the same purposes. Skins, generally goat but sometimes sheep or gazelle, were turned into bags, pouches, wallets, tent covers, cushions, cords, and containers for storing water, milk, and butter. Today artisans continue to make leather bags and other pieces in traditional forms while also creating purses and other accessories for non-Tuareg buyers.

Whereas male artisans specialize in metalwork and woodwork, leatherworking is the domain of female members of the artisan class (*tineden*). To work goat or other animal skins, they soak the skins in water and

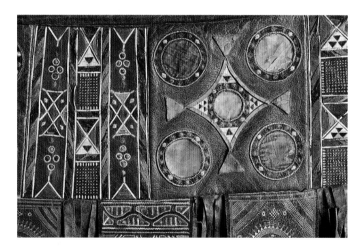

remove the hair, then tan them in vegetable tannins and soften them with butter or oil. The colored leather found frequently in appliqué designs is dyed with mineral or chemical dyes, most often in green, black, white, yellow, and red. Women decorate leather bags and wallets using a wide variety of techniques, including painting, embroidery, colored leather appliqué, and incising of geometric designs, all of which can be seen on this magnificently decorated leather bag.

Kel Ahaggar women used this type of large bag to store clothing, jewelry, and other personal items. It hung from one side of the camel saddle when the owner traveled and on a tent post on the women's side of the tent when the group was camped. The opening at the top could be secured with a metal lock (pl. 22) by inserting the bar of the lock in the holes punched along the bag's top opening. Making a bag like this one was an activity shared by a number of women and might take months to complete. (Opposite: 98520093; above: portion of decorated under-flap, detail of 98520092. Mark Craig, photographer.)

Man's leather bag
61-32-50/10459
Algerian Sahara
Leather, cotton
54.5 × 26 × 1.3 cm
Collected by Maurice Reygasse,
1912–1930; donated by Lloyd Cabot
Briggs in 1961

MEMBERS OF THE TUAREG NOBLE CLASSES generally did not make the beautifully decorated objects they used but acquired them from *ineden*. These artisans usually lived in agricultural centers and were associated with particular noble groups who camped in territory nearby. Today most artisans live in towns or cities, where they sell their products to both Tuareg and non-Tuareg clients. In addition to acquiring objects from local *ineden*, the Kel Ahaggar Tuareg living in Algeria also obtained goods from artisans in market centers such as Agadez in northern Niger. Some of these artisans were Berber speakers associated with Tuareg groups, but Hausa artisans and traders also supplied many objects to the Kel Ahaggar. The most prestigious type of indigo-dyed fabric for the *tagelmust* turban and face veil, for example, was produced by Hausa artisans and sold by Hausa traders living in market centers.

The red embroidered circles on this bag were originally distinguishing traits of Hausa women's work, and the bright green leather used in the appliqué designs was a specialty of Agadez, where a local source of copper provided the green dye. These motifs are commonly found on the large leather traveling bags used by Tuareg men, and in 1947 French explorer and collector Henri Lhote wrote that Hausa women "have the monopoly on [the] fabrication" of such bags. Large traveling bags decorated in this style, he said, were used only by the Tuareg and were one of their "most classic" types of camel trappings.[89] (T4836.3. Hillel S. Burger, photographer.)

Notes

1. My main source for standard English spellings of geographical names is Saul Bernard Cohen and Columbia University Press, *The Columbia Gazetteer of the World* [electronic resource] (New York: Columbia University Press, 2001). For the orthography and English translations of Berber words I have relied on Gabriel Camps, "Note sur la transcription," in *Encyclopédie Berbère*, vol. 1, ed. Gabriel Camps (Aix-en-Provence, France: Edisud, 1984); Jean-Marie Dallet, *Dictionnaire Kabyle-Français* (Paris: SELAF [Société d'Etudes Linguistiques et Anthropologiques de France], 1982); David M. Hart, *The Aith Waryaghar of the Moroccan Rif: An Ethnography and History* (Tucson: University of Arizona Press, 1976); Jeremy Keenan, *The Lesser Gods of the Sahara: Social Change and Contested Terrain amongst the Tuareg of Algeria* (London: Frank Cass, 2004); and Thomas K. Seligman and Kristyne Loughran, eds., *Art of Being Tuareg: Sahara Nomads in a Modern World* (Los Angeles: UCLA Fowler Museum of Cultural History, 2006).

2. The Peabody also houses small collections of Berber art from the High Atlas Mountains of Morocco, from the M'zab region in the northern Sahara of Algeria, and from Tuareg areas in Niger and Mali. Some items in the Peabody's North African collections are not from Berber-speaking regions, notably examples of urban dress from Morocco and Algeria.

3. See Michael Brett and Elizabeth Fentress, *The Berbers* (Oxford: Blackwell, 1996) for an excellent overview of Berber history, from which much of this section is drawn. Also of interest for general information on the Berbers is Gabriel Camps, *Les Berbères: Mémoire et identité*, 3rd ed. (Paris: Editions Errance, 1995).

4. Statistics taken from Brett and Fentress, *The Berbers, 3*, and Salem Chaker, *Berbères aujourd'hui: Berbères dans le Maghreb contemporain*, 2nd ed. (Paris: L'Harmattan, 1998), 14–15, 49.

5. Mutual comprehensibility depends on factors including geographical distance between the varieties and the experience of individual speakers. An article by a Berber activist from Kabylia who visited the oasis of Siwa in Egypt, the easternmost Berber-speaking population in North Africa, suggests that even such geographically separated dialects can be understood with a bit of practice, but this is certainly not always the case. See Belkacem Lounes, *L'Oasis de Siwa: Une légende à l'autre bout de Tamazgha?* (1999), www.mondeberbere.com/PARImazigh/ Parimazigh5/siwa.htm.

6. The words *At, Aith, Ait, Axt,* and *Kel* mean "people of" in different Berber varieties. They are used to form tribal or regional names, making the At Yenni "the people of Yenni." Nineteenth- and early-twentieth-century writers also used *Beni*, a version of the equivalent Arabic term, to form Berber tribal names. In this book I follow current usage for transcribing these terms in the appropriate Berber variety but leave the Arabic versions when they are quoted from other writers' texts.

7. "Amazigh art" is not a category the original makers and users of these pieces would have used. The objects would most likely have been described in terms of locally specific styles— jewelry from the At Yenni, for example. The museum's collection allows one to bring together objects produced in geographically dispersed regions to examine them in terms of a pan-regional aesthetic.

8. See James Bynon, "Berber Women's Pottery: Is the Decoration Motivated?" in *Earthenware in Asia and Africa*, ed. John Picton (London: Percival David Foundation of Chinese Art, 1984), and Moira Vincentelli, "Reflections on a Kabyle Pot: Algerian Women and the Decorative Tradition," *Journal of Design History* 2, no. 2–3 (1989): 123–138, for a discussion of this issue in relation to pottery traditions. See Francis Ramirez and Christian Rolot, *Tapis et tissages du Maroc: Une écriture du silence* (Paris: ACR Edition Internationale, 1995) in relation to textiles. Niloo Imami Paydar and Ivo Grammet, eds., *The Fabric of Moroccan Life* (Indianapolis: Indianapolis Museum of Art, 2002), and Beatrice Riottot El-Habib and Marie-France Vivier, eds., *Algérie: Mémoire de femmes au fil des doigts* (Paris: Somogy Editions d'Art, 2003), both give good overviews of Berber symbology.

9. See Cynthia Becker, *Amazigh Arts in Morocco: Women Shaping Berber Identity* (Austin: University of Texas Press, 2006), for a recent study that develops these themes.

10. See Bynon, "Berber Women's Pottery," for a discussion of the history of belief in the evil eye and protective measures against it in North Africa. Also see John Mack, ed., *Africa: Arts and Cultures* (London: British Museum Press, 2000), 50–53.

11. Edward Westermarck, *Ritual and Belief in Morocco*, vol. 1 (London: Macmillan, 1926), 452–467. Bynon, in "Berber Women's Pottery," argued that Westermarck might have been reading too much into some of these symbols.

12. Bynon, "Berber Women's Pottery," 145; Kristyne Loughran, "Jewelry, Fashion, and Identity: The Tuareg Example," *African Arts* 36, no. 1 (2003): 52–65.

13. See Brett and Fentress, *The Berbers*, chapter 7, for recent scholarship on Berber tribal government, and Patricia M. E. Lorcin, *Imperial Identities: Stereotyping, Prejudice, and Race in Colonial Algeria* (New York: I. B. Tauris, 1999), on the "Kabyle myth" constructed by French colonial scholars of the region. Information on the general history of Kabylia is also taken from Ali Marok and Tahar Djaout, *La Kabylie* (Paris: Paris-Méditerranée, 1997). Jane E. Goodman, *Berber Culture on the World Stage: From Village to Video* (Bloomington: Indiana University Press, 2005), offers many insights into life in Kabylia today.

14. See Charles-Robert Ageron, *Modern Algeria: A History from 1830 to the Present*, trans. Michael Brett (Trenton, NJ: Africa World Press, 1991), on Kabyle resistance to French colonial rule. See Benjamin Stora, "Figures Kabyles dans l'histoire politique algérienne," *Awal: Cahiers d'Etudes Berbères*, no. 25 (2002): 44–47, on Kabyle participation in the Algerian war for independence. For an overview of the Amazigh cultural movement, see Brett and Fentress, *The Berbers*, chapter 8.

15. Robert Lambert Playfair, *Murray's Handbook for Travellers in Algeria and Tunis* (London: John Murray, 1878), 4. Information on tourism in Algeria and Kabylia in the late nineteenth century is taken primarily from English-language travel guides such as this one, which would have been used by American visitors to Algeria. See George W. Harris, *"The" Practical Guide to Algiers*, 3rd ed. (London: George Philip and Son, 1893); Joseph C. Hyam, *The Illustrated Guide to Algiers: A "Practical" Handbook for Travellers*, 6th ed. (Algiers: Anglo-French Press Association, 1908); and Thomas Cook and Son, *Cook's Practical Guide to Algiers, Algeria and Tunisia: With Maps, Plans, and Illustrations* (London: Thomas Cook and Son, 1903).

16. Harris, *"The" Practical Guide*, 93–94.

17. Among the objects from Kabylia in the Peabody Museum's collections are also two baskets. One of these was collected by Mrs. William R. Castle, Jr., in Fort National (Larbaa Naït Irathen) around 1912; the other was part of a large collection of basketry from around the

world donated by Miss Lucy Eaton in 1932. The latter basket dates to 1908 or earlier.

18. Peabody Museum Accession File 04-22.

19. Museum of Fine Arts Boston, *Annual Report*, 1878, 1890; Museum of Fine Arts Boston, *Ninth Catalogue of the Collection of Ancient and Modern Works of Art*, 1878. The Peabody Museum's 1904 accession from the Museum of Fine Arts included six pieces of pottery labeled "Kabyle," but they are not typical of the Kabyle region. Perhaps these were the "Moorish" pottery pieces donated to the Museum of Fine Arts by Thornton K. Lothrop. The words *Moors* and *Moorish* were used at the time to refer to the populations of North African cities, people of various descents who led urban lives, as opposed to their rural Arab or Berber counterparts.

20. Biographical information on Thornton Kirkland Lothrop and Algernon Coolidge is taken from *The National Cyclopaedia of American Biography*, vols. 14:225–226 (1910) and 29: 304–305 (1941) (New York: J. T. White).

21. Peabody Museum Catalogue Cards 42-23 and 31-27.

22. Peabody Museum Catalogue Cards 36-107, 36-112, and 41-34.

23. These photographs were part of a genre of professional photographs of Algerian "scenes and types" that were distributed in large printed formats as well as in postcard form. See Malek Alloula, *The Colonial Harem*, trans. Wlad Godzich and Myrna Godzich (Minneapolis: University of Minnesota Press, 1986); and Leila Sebbar and Jean-Michel Belorgey, *Femmes d'Afrique du Nord: Cartes postales* (1885–1930) (Saint-Pourçin-sur-Sioule: Bleu Autour, 2002).

24. All information on Bowditch's travels in Algeria is from letters in the Charles P. Bowditch family papers at the Massachusetts Historical Society.

25. Charles P. Bowditch to Lucy Rockwell Bowditch, Fort National, 10 January 1902, Charles P. Bowditch family papers, Massachusetts Historical Society.

26. Cornelia Bowditch to Lucy Rockwell Bowditch, Algiers, 26 January 1902, Charles P. Bowditch family papers, Massachusetts Historical Society.

27. Adolphe Hanoteau and Aristide Horace Letourneux, *La Kabylie et les coutumes kabyles* (Paris: Imprimerie Nationale, 1872).

28. Information on Kabyle pottery manufacture and designs in this chapter and in the plates is taken from Hélène Balfet, "La poterie des Aït Smaïl du Djurdjura: Éléments d'étude esthé-tique," *Revue Africaine* 99 (1955): 289–340; Arnold van Gennep, *Études d'ethnographie algéri-enne: Les soufflets algériens—Les poteries kabyles—Le tissage aux cartons—L'art décoratif* (Paris: E. Leroux, 1911); Bynon, "Berber Women's Pottery"; and El-Habib and Vivier, *Algérie*. A brief but informative piece on Kabyle pottery can be found in Mack, *Africa: Arts and Cultures*, 56–57. Vincentelli, "Reflections on a Kabyle Pot," provides information on more recent forms of Kabyle pottery.

29. Hanoteau and Letourneux, *La Kabylie et les coutumes kabyles*, 472.

30. Information on Kabyle costume and textile traditions here and in the plates is from Leyla Belkaid, *Costumes d'Algérie* (Paris: Editions du Layeur, 2003); Germaine Laoust-Chantréaux, *Kabylie côté femmes: La vie féminine à Aït Hichem*, 1937–39 (Aix-en-Provence: Edisud, 1990); Germaine Chantréaux, "Les tissages sur métier de haute lisse à Ait-Hichem et dans le Haut Sebaou," *Revue Africaine*, published serially in issues 386–387, 388–389, and 392–393, in 1941–1942; and John Picton and John Mack, *African Textiles: Looms, Weaving and Design* (London: British Museum, 1979).

31. Information on Kabyle jewelry here and in the plates is from Tatiana Benfoughal, ed., *Bijoux et parures d'Algérie: Histoire, techniques, symboles* (Paris: Somogy Editions d'Art, 2003); Henriette Camps-Fabrer, *Les Bijoux de Grande Kabylie: Collections du Musée du Bardo et du Centre de Recherches Anthropologiques, Préhistoriques et Ethnographiques, Alger* (Paris: Arts et Métiers Graphiques, 1970); and Wassyla Tamzali, *Abzim: Parures et bijoux des femmes d'Algérie* (Paris: Dessain et Tolra, 1984).

32. Carleton S. Coon, *Tribes of the Rif* (Cambridge, MA: Peabody Museum of Harvard University, 1931); David M. Hart, *Tribe and Society in Rural Morocco* (London: Frank Cass, 2000). Information on the history and society of the Rif are taken from Coon, *Tribes of the Rif*; Hart, *Aith Waryaghar*; and David Seddon, *Moroccan Peasants: A Century of Change in the Eastern Rif, 1870–1970* (Folkestone, UK: Dawson, 1981).

33. See David McMurray, *In and Out of Morocco: Smuggling and Migration in a Frontier Boomtown* (Minneapolis: University of Minnesota Press, 2001), for more on migration and trade in one town in northern Morocco. See Pierre-Arnaud Chouvy, "Morocco Said to Produce Nearly Half the World's Hashish Supply," *Jane's Intelligence Review* 17, no. 11 (2005): 32–35, on cannabis production.

34. Carleton S. Coon, *Flesh of the Wild Ox: A Riffian Chronicle of High Valleys and Long Rifles* (London: Jonathan Cape, 1932); Carleton S. Coon, *The Riffian* (London: Jonathan Cape, 1934).

35. Carleton S. Coon, *Adventures and Discoveries: The Autobiography of Carleton S. Coon* (Englewood Cliffs, NJ: Prentice-Hall, 1981); Carleton S. Coon, *A North Africa Story: The Anthropologist as OSS Agent, 1941–1943* (Ipswich, MA: Gambit, 1980).

36. Carleton S. Coon, *Caravan: The Story of the Middle East* (New York: Henry Holt, 1951); Carleton S. Coon, *The Story of Man: From the First Human to Primitive Culture and Beyond* (New York: Knopf, 1954).

37. See Franz Boas, *A Franz Boas Reader: The Shaping of American Anthropology, 1883–1911*, ed. George W. Stocking, Jr. (Chicago: University of Chicago Press, Midway Reprint, 1989), 189–254.

38. See Pat Shipman, *The Evolution of Racism: Human Differences and the Use and Abuse of Science* (New York: Simon and Schuster, 1994), for a good overview of scientific studies of race and a balanced exposition of the bitter controversy that erupted over Coon's conclusions in his 1962 book *The Origin of Races* (New York: Knopf). The original debate, including Coon's response, can be found in Theodosius Dobzhansky, Ashley Montagu, and Carleton S. Coon, "Two Views of Coon's *Origin of Races* with Comments by Coon and Replies," *Current Anthropology* 4, no. 4 (1963): 360–367.

39. Coon, *Adventures*, 27. Information on Carleton Coon's research in Morocco is taken from his autobiography as well as from unpublished letters and field notes housed in the Carleton S. Coon Papers at the National Anthropological Archives, Smithsonian Institution.

40. Carleton Coon to Earnest Hooton, Casablanca, 15 August 1925, Carleton S. Coon Papers (Box 17), National Anthropological Archives, Smithsonian Institution. "Shawia" here refers to an Arabic-speaking tribe near Casablanca. It is also the name of the Berbers inhabiting the Aurès region of northeastern Algeria (also spelled Chaouia).

41. The sheikh's father, Hajj Muhand Biqqish, was described by David Hart as the main leader of Riffian resistance forces in his region. Hart, *Aith Waryaghar*, 368.

42. Coon, *Adventures*, 44.

43. Coon, *Tribes of the Rif,* viii. Coon collected blood samples from the men he measured in order to establish whether or not a correlation existed between blood type and other physical characteristics.

44. Coon, *Adventures*, 64.

45. Ibid., 67.

46. Information on Riffian women's pottery traditions, here and in the plates, is taken primarily from André Bazzana, Rahma Elhraiki, and Yves Montmessin, *La mémoire du geste: La poterie féminine et domestique du Rif marocain* (Paris: Maisonneuve and Larose, 2003).

47. Brett and Fentress, *The Berbers*, 260–262.

48. This gender division in decoration clearly does not apply to all North African pottery. The urban ceramic industries of Morocco combine industrial production and elaborate painted designs. There are also examples of rural men's pottery that do make use of decoration. See Bernd Hakenjos, *Marokkanische Keramik* (Stuttgart: H. Mayer, 1988), for some examples, as well as a description of a potter in the Zerhoun region who made pottery explicitly intended to echo women's pottery traditions. Exactly where Coon and Browne's pieces fit into this picture is unclear. The pieces were purchased in the Zerhoun region, outside of Meknes, and were said to have been made by members of the Axt Tuzin, a Riffian tribe that had settled there in the late nineteenth century. The women of this tribe made painted pottery similar to that of the

central Rif. See Marie-Barthélémy-Joseph Herber, "Technique des poteries rifaines du Zerhoun," *Hesperis* 2, no. 3 (1922): 241–253. The men of this tribe, according to Coon, also made pottery meant to imitate Riffian women's pottery (see pl. 13). The question is also complicated by the presence of stickers reading "Made in Morocco" on the bottoms of many of these pieces. This might indicate that they were made to be sold to tourists, but it does not necessarily do so.

49. Hart, *Aith Waryaghar*, 45.

50. The Peabody Museum has also benefited from the generosity of later donors of Tuareg art objects, among them Robin and Kendall Mix and Dr. Mark Rapoport. These donors have supplemented Briggs's collection by providing pieces from other regions inhabited by Tuareg groups, notably Niger and Mali. These pieces (pls. 17, 21, 23) showcase some of the distinct regional styles found in Tuareg art.

51. For general information on the Tuareg and an excellent treatment of their artisanship today, see Seligman and Loughran, *Art of Being Tuareg*. Information on Kel Ahaggar history and society is from Jeremy Keenan, *The Tuareg: People of Ahaggar* (London: Sickle Moon Books, 2002); and Keenan, *Lesser Gods of the Sahara*. Many of the political, social, and economic structures described here apply to other Tuareg groups as well, but I focus on the Kel Ahaggar because they were the group from which Briggs acquired most of his collections.

52. Unless they are religiously conservative, women in many Berber regions of North Africa do not generally cover their faces either, although, like Tuareg women, they might do so in certain social contexts.

53. See Keenan, *Lesser Gods*, chapter 4, for a discussion of the complex meanings and practices associated with the *tagelmust* and the factors behind the decline in its use among the Kel Ahaggar today. Keenan notes that a similar decline has not taken place to the same extent in the Tuareg regions of Mali and Niger.

54. Like much else in "traditional" Tuareg society, this has changed significantly in the past forty years. See *Lesser Gods*, chapter 5.

55. See Seligman and Loughran, *Art of Being Tuareg*, especially chapters 3, 4, and 8, for insights into the roles of Tuareg artisans and the ways their lives have changed in recent years.

56. Keenan, *Lesser Gods*, 166.

57. Lloyd Cabot Briggs, *Tribes of the Sahara* (Cambridge, MA: Harvard University Press, 1960), xix; and see Lloyd Cabot Briggs, *The Living Races of the Sahara Desert*, Papers of the Peabody Museum of Archaeology and Ethnology, Harvard University, vol. 28, no. 2 (Cambridge, MA: Peabody Museum, 1958).

58. Lloyd Cabot Briggs and Norina Lami Guède, *No More For Ever: A Saharan Jewish Town*,

Papers of the Peabody Museum of Archaeology and Ethnology, Harvard University, vol. 55, no. 1 (1964).

59. Lloyd Cabot Briggs, "Biographical Summary, Harvard College Class of 1931," in *Thirty-fifth Anniversary Report* (Cambridge, MA: Harvard Development Office, 1966). Biographical information about Briggs is taken from this report as well as from biographical summaries he submitted to the Class of 1931 in 1941, 1946, and 1956.

60. Some of these photos were published in Alexander Campbell, "Africa: A Continent in Ferment," *Life*, May 4, 1953, 36–38. See also David Douglas Duncan, *Yankee Nomad: A Photographic Odyssey* (New York: Holt, Rinehart and Winston, 1966), 356–359. David Douglas Duncan kindly provided information about this trip.

61. Lloyd Cabot Briggs, "European Blades in Tuareg Swords and Daggers," *Journal of the Arms and Armour Society* 5, no. 2 (1965): 37–95.

62. Briggs, *Tribes of the Sahara*, viii.

63. Musée du Bardo Algiers, *Collections Ethnographiques, Touareg Ahaggar* (Paris: Arts et Métiers Graphiques, 1959).

64. See El-Habib and Vivier, *Algérie*, for Tuareg objects in the collections of the Musée du Quai Branly and Algerian museums; Jean Gabus, *Au Sahara: Arts et symboles* (Neuchâtel: À la Baconnière, 1955); and Jan-B. Cuypers, ed., *Touareg: Album de photographies et catalogue de l'exposition, Tervuren, 4 mars–31 juillet 1994* (Tervuren, Belgium: Musée Royal de l'Afrique Centrale, 1994).

65. Musée du Bardo Algiers, *Collections Ethnographiques*, pl. 1.

66. For good overviews of Tuareg arts and artisanship, see Seligman and Loughran, *Art of Being Tuareg*; Johannes Nicolaisen and Ida Nicolaisen, *The Pastoral Tuareg: Ecology, Culture and Society* (London: Thames and Hudson, 1997); and Cuypers, *Touareg*. Much information on specific object types both here and in the plates is taken from Seligman and Loughran, *Art of Being Tuareg*; Musée du Bardo Algiers, *Collections Ethnographiques*; and Marceau Gast, "Aspects de l'artisanat chez les Kel Ahaggar en 1953," *Libyca* 11 (1963): 221–233.

67. For more on Tuareg weaponry, see Briggs, "European Blades," and Christopher Spring, *African Arms and Armour* (London: British Museum Press, 1993), 27–30.

68. Information on Tuareg jewelry, here and in the plates, is from Seligman and Loughran, *Art of Being Tuareg*, chapter 7; Loughran, "Jewelry, Fashion, and Identity"; Jean Gabus, Hans Erni, and Walter Hugentobler, *Sahara: Bijoux et techniques* (Neuchâtel: À la Baconnière, 1982); and Tamzali, *Abzim*.

69. See Seligman and Loughran, *Art of Being Tuareg*, chapter 9, for an account of the origins of the cross pendant and the multiple uses of the "cross of Agadez" today.

70. For discussions of contemporary artists on which much of this chapter is based, see Becker, *Amazigh Arts in Morocco*, chapter 7, and Cynthia Becker, "Contemporary Moroccan and Algerian Painters: Custodians of Amazigh Consciousness," in *North African Mosaic: A Cultural Reappraisal of Ethnic and Religious Minorities*, eds. Nabil Boudraa and Joseph Krause (Newcastle, UK: Cambridge Scholars Publishing, 2007), 271–292.

71. Brett and Fentress, *The Berbers*, 37.

72. Translated into French by Adolphe Hanoteau from a transcription of a stone bracelet from Algeria. Quoted in Henri Lhote, "L'anneau de bras des Touareg, ses techniques et ses rapports avec la préhistoire," *Bulletin de l'Institut Français d'Afrique Noire* 12, no. 2 (1950): 484. Translation from French by the author.

73. Peabody Museum Accession File 969-16.

74. Coon, *Adventures*, 63.

75. Westermarck, *Ritual and Belief in Morocco*, 452–467.

76. Peabody Museum Accession File 54-42.

77. Quotations here and in plate 11 are from Charles P. Bowditch to Lucy Rockwell Bowditch, Fort National, 10 January 1902, Charles P. Bowditch family papers, Massachusetts Historical Society. Bowditch probably meant that the man had participated in the World's Columbian Exposition, held in Chicago in 1893. Apparently it was not uncommon for Kabyle artisans to participate in international expositions. Anthony Wilkin, during a journey into Kabylia in 1900, mentioned meeting artisans who had sent their woodwork to the 1900 Exposition Universelle in Paris. Anthony Wilkin, *Among the Berbers of Algeria* (London: T. Fisher Unwin, 1900).

78. Hyam, *Illustrated Guide*, 129.

79. Carleton S. Coon, "Riffian Trip Reports," Ajdir, 26 December 1926, Carleton S. Coon Papers (Box 43), National Anthropological Archives, Smithsonian Institution. Other provenance information on Coon's collection also comes from his unpublished field notes and letters.

80. Coon, *Tribes of the Rif*, 75.

81. Coon, *Adventures*, 63.

82. Carleton S. Coon, "Riffian Trip Reports," Suk es-Sebt, Gzennaya, 4 September 1927, Carleton S. Coon Papers (Box 43), National Anthropological Archives, Smithsonian Institution.

83. See Westermarck, *Ritual and Belief in Morocco*, 436–443, on the use of charms to defend against the evil eye.

84. See Labelle Prussin, *African Nomadic Architecture: Space, Place, and Gender* (Washington, DC: Smithsonian Institution Press, 1995), 88–101, and Seligman and Loughran, *Art of Being Tuareg*, 90–93, for information on the Tuareg tent.

85. Peabody Museum of Archaeology and Ethnology, *Report on the Peabody Museum of Archaeology and Ethnology*, 1941–59 (1959).

86. See Jean Gabus, *Arts et symboles* (Neuchâtel: À la Baconnière, 1958), 233–235.

87. Ibid., 226. Translation from French by the author. The *ahal* is a gathering for reciting poetry, performing music, and engaging in poetic competitions that is part of Tuareg courtship. See Seligman and Loughran, *Art of Being Tuareg*, 51; Brett and Fentress, *The Berbers*, 213.

88. Peabody Museum Accession File 975-69 and 985-17.

89. Henri Lhote, *Comment campent les Touaregs: Ouvrage accompagné de 97 photos, de l'auteur et avec la collaboration du Service du dessin du Musée de l'homme* (Paris: J. Susse, 1947), 142.

Suggested Reading

Much of the literature on Amazigh arts and culture is in French, and I direct readers to the notes for detailed studies of specific regions and types of objects. Following are some English-language publications on North African and Berber history, arts, and culture and some references for the two main collectors of the Peabody Museum's Berber objects.

Becker, Cynthia
2006   *Amazigh Arts in Morocco: Gendered Symbols of Ethnic Identity*. Austin: University of Texas Press.
         An exploration of Berber women's arts and ethnic identity in southeastern Morocco, based on historical sources and recent fieldwork. Includes discussions of dress, textiles, wedding practices, songs, dances, and contemporary Amazigh arts.

Brett, Michael, and Elizabeth Fentress
1996   *The Berbers*. Oxford: Blackwell.
         A comprehensive introduction to Berber history and culture, starting with the earliest evidence of humans in North Africa and following the course of Berber history through antiquity, the coming of Islam, and the colonial and post-independence periods.

Briggs, Lloyd Cabot

1960   *Tribes of the Sahara.* Cambridge, MA: Harvard University Press.

Presents physical, social, linguistic, and cultural information about the Saharan Berber and non-Berber peoples, based on Briggs's thorough reading of the written sources and his own field research. Written for a general audience. The chapter on the Tuareg is an absorbing account of Tuareg life in the mid-twentieth century.

Coon, Carleton S.

1931   *Tribes of the Rif.* Cambridge, MA: Peabody Museum of Harvard University.

A report of Coon's fieldwork in Morocco from 1926 to 1928, offering a holistic view of the Riffian tribes in the early twentieth century. Also of interest are Coon's novels about the Rif, *Flesh of the Wild Ox* (1932) and *The Riffian* (1934).

1980   *A North Africa Story: The Anthropologist as OSS Agent, 1941–1943.* Ipswich, MA: Gambit.

1981   *Adventures and Discoveries: The Autobiography of Carleton S. Coon.* Englewood Cliffs, NJ: Prentice-Hall.

Two autobiographical works telling the stories of Coon's service with the Office of Strategic Services in World War II and his research and travels in Morocco and many other parts of the world. Coon's lively writing style makes for entertaining reading.

Courtney-Clarke, Margaret, and Geraldine Brooks

1996   *Imazighen: The Vanishing Traditions of Berber Women.* New York: Clarkson Potter.

Stunning photographs of Berber regions in Morocco, Algeria, and Tunisia, with a special focus on women and women's arts. The photographs are accompanied by essays by Geraldine Brooks.

Goodman, Jane E.

2005   *Berber Culture on the World Stage: From Village to Video.* Bloomington: Indiana University Press.

An ethnography of Berber culture with a special focus on the world music genre known as new Kabyle song. On the basis of recent fieldwork in Kabylia and France, Goodman traces the historical and contemporary formation of Berber cultural identity.

Hagan, Helene

2006   *Tuareg Jewelry: Traditional Patterns and Symbols*. Philadelphia: Xlibris.
Investigates Tuareg art forms from prehistoric rock art to modern jewelry designs.
Written in collaboration with Berber artists and specialists in Morocco and Niger.

Hart, David M.

2000   *Tribe and Society in Rural Morocco*. London: Frank Cass.
Essays reflecting on Hart's many years of research and writing about Berber regions
of Morocco, including the Rif and the Ait Atta tribal areas of the south-central Atlas
Mountains.

Hoffman, Katherine E.

2007   *We Share Walls: Language, Land, and Gender in Berber Morocco*. Oxford: Blackwell.
An ethnography of language, gender, and ethnic identity based on fieldwork in
southern Morocco.

Jereb, James F.

1995   *Arts and Crafts of Morocco*. San Francisco: Chronicle Books.
An overview of rural and urban arts of Morocco. Arts of Berber regions are well represented in color photographs and essays that address techniques of manufacture as
well as symbols and beliefs surrounding artistic production.

Keenan, Jeremy

2002   *The Tuareg: People of Ahaggar*. London: Sickle Moon Books.
A study of the Kel Ahaggar Tuareg based on research carried out in the years following Algerian independence in 1962. Keenan provides a historical account of Kel
Ahaggar society before and during French colonial rule and examines the profound
changes brought about by post-independence state policies.

2004   *The Lesser Gods of the Sahara: Social Change and Contested Terrain amongst the Tuareg of
Algeria*. London: Frank Cass.
Essays describing the social and economic conditions of the Kel Ahaggar Tuareg as
observed after Keenan's return to the Ahaggar region in 1999, for the first time in
more than 20 years.

Mack, John, ed.

2000   *Africa: Arts and Cultures*. London: British Museum Press.
        Covers the British Museum's African collections and includes a significant section
        on North Africa, giving historical background as well as technical, aesthetic, and
        symbolic analyses. The color plates are accompanied by brief essays by scholars
        prominent in the field of North African arts.

Paydar, Niloo Imami, and Ivo Grammet, eds.

2002   *The Fabric of Moroccan Life*. Indianapolis: Indianapolis Museum of Art.
        Catalogue of an exhibition held at the Indianapolis Museum of Art in 2002 display-
        ing Moroccan textiles from rural and urban areas. The section on rural weavings
        includes an overview of techniques and designs and in-depth essays on textiles from
        many Berber-speaking regions.

Saulniers, Alfred, and Suzanne Saulniers

2003   *Ait Bou Ichaouen: Weavings of a Nomadic Berber Tribe*. Tucson, AZ: Fenestra Books.
        Presents the weavings of one Berber-speaking group living in the foothills of the
        Atlas Mountains in Morocco, providing detailed information on techniques of man-
        ufacture and an analysis of weaving motifs specific to this region.

Seligman, Thomas K., and Kristyne Loughran, eds.

2006   *Art of Being Tuareg: Sahara Nomads in a Modern World*. Los Angeles: UCLA Fowler
        Museum of Cultural History.
        Brings together essays from American, European, and Tuareg scholars focusing on
        Tuareg life and arts today. Offers much information on genres of dress, jewelry,
        music, and other arts, including techniques of manufacture, the lives of Tuareg arti-
        sans, and Tuareg aesthetics.

Spring, Christopher, and Julie Hudson

1995   *North African Textiles*. Washington, DC: Smithsonian Institution Press.
        Presents textiles from rural and urban areas across North Africa, devoting special
        attention to the historical developments and diverse traditions that have affected
        textile arts. Includes sections on materials and weaving techniques, patterns and
        symbols, modes of dress, and contemporary production.